T0371806

Achieving Successful and Sustainable Project Delivery in Africa

Achieving Successful and Sustainable Project Delivery in Africa

How to Implement Effective and Efficient Project Management Practices and Policies

Dr. Okoro Chima Okereke

Routledge
Taylor & Francis Group

A PRODUCTIVITY PRESS BOOK

First published 2020
by Routledge
52 Vanderbilt Avenue, New York, NY 10017

and by Routledge
2 Park Square, Milton Park, Abingdon, Oxon, OX14 4RN
Routledge is an imprint of the Taylor & Francis Group, an informa business

Library of Congress Cataloging-in-Publication Data
Names: Okereke, Chima, 1946- author.
Title: Achieving successful and sustainable project delivery in Africa :
how to implement effective and efficient project management practices
and policies / Okoro Chima Okereke.
Description: New York, NY : Routledge, 2020. | Includes bibliographical
references and index.
Identifiers: LCCN 2019057037 (print) | LCCN 2019057038 (ebook) | ISBN
9780367437626 (hardback) | ISBN 9781003006268 (ebook)
Subjects: LCSH: Project management--Africa. | Sustainable
development--Africa.
Classification: LCC HD69.P75 O54 2020 (print) | LCC HD69.P75 (ebook) |
DDC 363.6068/4--dc23
LC record available at https://lccn.loc.gov/2019057037
LC ebook record available at https://lccn.loc.gov/2019057038

ISBN: 978-0-367-43762-6 (hbk)
ISBN: 978-1-003-00626-8 (ebk)

Typeset in Garamond
by Deanta Global Publishing Services, Chennai, India

To:

My father: Late Mazi Isaac Ukpo Okereke

My mother: Late Madam Mabel Ogbonneya Okereke

My wife: Dr. Catherine Nnenna Chima-Okereke

Our children: Chibisi

Chidinma

Onyekachi

Onyinyechi

Uchechi

Contents

Preface

I have been interested in writing and equally keen to contribute to addressing the problems that militate against the development of Africa. It is little wonder that for about 16 years, since 2003, I started writing my company newsletter on best practices and developments in project management as a tool to help enlighten our customers on the benefits of structured project management.

Some four years later, I met David Pells, the managing editor of *PM World* at a PMI Global Congress at Anaheim. He suggested that I should start writing for his journal on project management issues in Nigeria. I began and continued for years, churning out various articles which he published, at least 30 in number.

In about 2016, he advised that it might be a good idea to collate my articles into a book. Another colleague of mine in Nigeria, who was an avid reader of my newsletters, also made the same suggestion about that time.

It was then that the idea of writing a book caught my interest. However, when I took it up, it was not just a collation of my past articles but a book that should be original and contribute to the solution of the problems that perpetuate under development in Africa. With time, I chose the title: *Achieving Successful and Sustainable Project Delivery in Africa.*

In 2017 and 2018, I was a speaker at a Pan-African Congress on Project Management. At the end of my presentation on each occasion, some members of the audience came to me asking for my book containing all these ideas. I knew that there had been a continuing demand for such a book, and I took to working on it, but not without much help from some project management professional colleagues.

Foreword

"It always seems impossible until it's done."

——**Nelson Mandela**

Why are projects important? Projects are the way organizations create products or services change organizations. It is through new products or services that organizations implement their strategy. An organization's strategy requires new products or services to deliver value to customers or to improve the processes in the organization. Or, stated another way, if an organization wants to implement its strategy, its products must deliver value to customers, and it is through projects that organizations can introduce or improve products.

For the past decade, the Project Management Institute (PMI) has been working hard to document the value of project management and how to improve project success. Studies done by the PMI and the Standish Group show that about one-third of projects are successful. However, PMI's research has found that if organizations improved their project management maturity, then two-thirds of projects are successful.

The conclusion is that organizations that want to successfully implement their strategy need to have a high level of project management maturity.

How do organizations improve their project management maturity? In my experience, there are three things you need to do. First, ensure that projects support the organization's strategy. Linking a project to the organization's strategy will ensure you get the resources you need to do the project as it is easy to demonstrate the benefit of doing the project. Second, use the right methodology to do the project. Organizations need to ensure they are doing the project the right way to ensure the project is successful. Third, ensure you have the right resources for the project, including a project manager with the required skills.

In this book, Dr. Okoro Chima Okereke brings focus for the need to improve project management in Africa. More importantly, Chima provides direction on how to improve project management maturity in Africa by using lessons learned on past project failures and implementing proven tools that have improved project management maturity in organizations around the world. The key is to select the right project, at the right time, do it the right way, and with the right resources.

Africa is full of opportunities and challenges, some of which I have witnessed on my visits to Africa. I hope that through this book and other initiatives, people and organizations in Africa can learn from the past to improve their project management maturity. Through improved project management maturity, organizations will be able to implement their strategy and achieve what seems to be impossible.

—Peter Monkhouse

Acknowledgements

I wish to start by thanking Peter Monkhouse, a past Chair of the Project Management Institute (PMI), and a top officer in PMI for many years, for accepting to read through the manuscript and then writing the foreword. Peter is a busy professional and leader in PMI. I am grateful that he made time for this.

Another PMI colleague, Darya Duma, was greatly supportive. She was the first peer to edit my initial manuscript and worked with me from 2018 until the manuscript was completed and submitted on 30 November 2019. Her advice at different times was invaluable. She encouraged me not only as a PMI colleague but also because she wanted something good for Africa. She was always interested in making her contributions to the development of project management in the continent including encouraging African professionals. I cannot thank her sufficiently for her efforts.

Professor Federico Minelle was another professional colleague, who worked as a peer reviewer from 2018. He had made such contributions that, when I thought that we needed four forewords, I invited him to write a foreword which he kindly did. However, our publishers use only one foreword and I did not know beforehand. I am thankful for his useful suggestions and contributions.

Dr. Lynn A. Keeys, President of PMI South Africa, was another peer reviewer. She received my initial manuscript in November 2018, about a year ago, and read through it. She also made some helpful criticisms and suggestions for which I am thankful.

Two other friends and professional colleagues also wrote respective forewords. Mr. Babbissakana, President of the Pan-African Project Management Conference, who invited me twice as a speaker at the conference in Yaoundé, wrote a beautiful foreword at my request – I thank him.

The second friend was my compatriot, and probably my longest acquaintance among these professional colleagues, Mr. Deji Ishmael. He was a founding member of PMI Lagos, a former Chapter President and PMI mentor for Africa Region. He also happily wrote a foreword, having known me for over 20 years as a PMI colleague from Nigeria. I am grateful for his support and for his many contributions to the development of project management in Africa.

Contributions were not only from PMI professionals but also from other professionals and officers in various capacities. For example, I am indebted to those who gladly permitted the use of their materials when I applied to do so. They include the following:

Ms. Ladi Olorunyomi, Editor, Washington, DC, Bureau of the Premium Times, who helped obtain the permission to use their investigation reports on the Nigerian Steel Industry.

Dr. Isaiah Damoah, a Lecturer in Project Management at the Bournemouth University, who easily gave me a free hand to use his survey report on Ghana as published in his PhD thesis.

Professors Keith Cattell, Paul Bowen and Peter Edwards who permitted me to use their investigation and survey report on the construction industry in South Africa.

Andrew Burger and the editors of *Africa Microgrid News* who easily granted me the permission to use their reports on the solar power industry in East Africa.

There are others, whose names cannot be listed here for space, who made various contributions. This book could not have been written in its present form without your various supports. I thank you all.

About the Author

Dr. Okoro Chima Okereke PhD, MBA, PMP, Senior Member IEEE, is the Managing Director of Total Technology Consultants, Ltd., a project and business management consulting company practising in Africa and the UK.

Pupil Engineering and Overseas Training

He started his career as a young electrical engineer in 1976 in Nigeria in the then National Electric Power Authority (NEPA) after completing his National Youth Corps Service (NYSC) and graduating from the University of Lagos, Nigeria. He had his initial hands-on training as a pupil engineer with technical assistants from Canadian Ontario Hydro in a number of electrical substations and electricity generating power stations comprising gas-fired power plants, steam thermal plants and coal-fired power plant, in Nigeria. He then had an in-depth hands-on overseas training with Electricity Supply Board of Ireland in Dublin and some other cities in Ireland for 13 months.

Industrial Career

In 1977, he returned to do further training with technical assistants from the then UK Central Electricity Generation Board (CEGB) and also participated in the installation, commissioning and operations of a 6 × 120 MW steam thermal power station at the NEPA Power Station, Ogorode, Sapele, Nigeria. He left NEPA as a Principal Engineer and Section Head for Instrumentation and Control. He worked briefly in Shell Petroleum Development Company in Warri as a technical trainer, a project engineer and writer in the Scallop Training Project between 1979 and 1982. In June 1982, he joined the Delta Steel Company Limited, Ovwian, Aladja, as a Deputy Manager. In 1984, he became a chief engineer and head of Instrumentation and Computing Systems.

He has been a Council for the Regulation of Engineering in Nigeria (COREN) registered engineer and a corporate member of the Nigerian

Society of Engineers since 1983 and 1982 respectively. He left the steel company for graduate studies in the UK in September 1988.

Graduate Studies in the UK

At the University of Bradford, West Yorkshire, England, he passed the taught part of the MBA degree in 1989. He obtained his PhD degree following research in robotics in 1994, and his Master's in Business Administration (MBA) degree following the successful completion of his dissertation in 1995.

Consulting Operations

Having established his company in the UK in 1995, he worked both in the UK and overseas. He also established a company in 2002 in Nigeria and worked as a Primavera Authorised Representative (PAR) serving, local, national and multinational companies. Between 2004 and 2008, on his initiative and working with the endorsement of Port Harcourt Chamber of Commerce, Industry, Mines and Agriculture (PHCCIMA), his company, which is Total Technology Consultants Limited, produced the first world-class Yellow Pages and Business Directory for the Rivers State of Nigeria. It is instructive that after this trailblazing publication, other entrepreneurs went on to produce their own versions of the Yellow Pages.

In June 2009, he took the PMI PMP certification examination and passed at the first attempt. Between 2002 and the end of 2018, his company trained over 600 project management professionals on enterprise project management courses in Nigeria and Gabon. His company was the first and only PAR in West Africa from 2003 to 2009. By 2019, it was a Gold-level member of Oracle Partner Network and also a partner of Microsoft, IBM and SAP.

Dr. Okoro Chima Okereke is a Visiting Professor, an industrial educator, a multidisciplinary project management professional and a specialist in industrial automation, with over 25 years of experience in oil and gas, steel and power generation industries. He is an international editorial adviser for the *PM World Journal* and *PM World Library*, having written over 30 published papers for the journal. He lives and works from his office in the UK and could be contacted at OkerekeOC@gmail.com, or chima.okereke@totaltechnologyconsultants.com.

Chapter 1

Introduction

It may be proper to introduce this book with a short list of data and observations on failed and abandoned projects in some African countries as given in the following paragraphs:

- In one country, a government commissioned audit revealed that 11,886 government projects failed in a period of 40 years up to 2011 (this translates to about 300 failed projects each year) [1].
- In October 2016, a former director-general of a government procurement unit in an African country stated that there were 19,000 government projects in various stages of abandonment [2].
- On 30 December 2011, citizens of a large African city were shocked when the government announced the failure and abandonment of a $10-billion housing project between the Government and a foreign company [3].
- It is sad that strategic industrial and scientific projects worth billions of dollars which were conceived with the best vision for the industrialisation of a country, were abandoned; some remain uncompleted after over ten years with much money sunk into the projects. The invested nation's resources and future industrialisation vision in the sector remained in tatters [4, 5].
- It has been the experience that new public enterprises appear to be generally implemented without any planned forecast of income generation from the project deliverables. These deliverables could be a government electricity generation plant, a steel production plant, a petroleum refinery, or any other government industrial plant, each of whose

project is planned, completed, commissioned and put into operation. Yet, there is no arrangement to ensure that the revenue generated will be adequate to fund the operations of the plant. Such revenue is required for salaries, cost of raw materials, cost of spare parts, cost of maintenance and replacement, etc. For example, in an African country, between 2010 and 2017, the Federal Government budgeted $66 million for a government owned steel company, out of which $62 million was used to pay salaries. The government kept allocating budget to pay workers' salaries to such companies which should have been able to generate funds for their operations but could not do so. The large industrial plants failed and were abandoned for many years. Some of the steel plants were being reactivated in 2018 and 2019 after over ten years of abandonment [6].

With this bleak failure picture, it is little wonder that our industrial landscape has become a "junkyard" of abandoned projects in various stages of disrepair and failure [7]. It is relevant to acknowledge that project failures and abandonment are not exclusive to African countries. Many countries, with well-developed economies, also experience project failures and abandonment. However, our continent is underdeveloped, and we are playing catch-up in economic development with advanced nations. We also lack the internal resources to help our catch-up efforts. In addition, our project failure rate is much higher than failure rates being experienced in developed countries. Therefore, we cannot continue to waste our scarce resources and those received from external investors.

It is necessary at this point to define the main words that will be encountered in the book, such as project failure, abandonment, successful, sustainable, corruption, etc.

Definition of Terms: Project Failure and Abandonment, Successful and Sustainable Project Delivery

Project failure and abandonment: Generally, when a project fails to deliver the agreed product or service on or within the agreed time or on or within budget, it is said to fail. However, even when the deliverables are produced with some over run on budget or time, organisations tend to accept the products or services. The focus of this book covers such projects which may not be completed and then abandoned, as well as project deliverables which cannot be operated after a few years of being produced. For example, they cannot be operated or used two or three years after production, and these are deliverables that should have a lifetime of over ten, twenty or more years. The emphasis is therefore on failed and abandoned projects.

Successful projects: These are projects that are generally completed on time and within budget and produce the agreed deliverables. Without being hard and fast over the precise completion on time and budget, some owners are happy to accept the project deliverables as long as they can keep them in operation over their planned lifetime.

Sustainable project delivery: This could be defined as the planning, monitoring and controlling of project delivery such that it considers and maintains the support processes, environment, financial returns, social and ethical impacts, and operations of the deliverables for the planned lifecycle of the project. It also considers the resources, processes, etc., in order to yield benefits for stakeholders.

This foregoing definition is helpful as a goal for the success being advocated in this book. It is sadly the case, as presented earlier in this introduction, that the current project delivery is so poor that many costly projects are abandoned and not completed. Some which are completed and produce deliverables are abandoned because there are no resources to sustain or maintain them in operations over their planned duration.

Corruption: This is a word that may occur as many as 65 times in this book. In its various manifestations in business, economics, politics, etc., it is blamed for most things that are badly handled. Whenever there is a failure of a project or even a public operation, the first reaction is to suspect corruption as the reason for it. This is the assumption even before the failure is investigated. According to Transparency International, corruption could be defined as "the abuse of entrusted power for private gain" [8].

Main Objective of the Book

The overriding objective of this book is to help prepare African public and private companies to conduct their projects effectively and efficiently so that they will successfully produce deliverables which are sustainable and can operate profitably throughout their planned lifetime. In other words, it should help achieve the following goals:

- New projects should be completed on time and on budget.
- Project deliverables should be operated competitively in the market. They should earn income to fund their operations and should be profitable throughout their planned lifetime.
- At the planning stage, there should be resources arrangement for the operation of the deliverable after it has been commissioned into service or production.
- There should be estimates of how much income the deliverable will generate during its lifetime operations including the benefits.
- There should be a timeline for the income to be produced.
- The income so generated should be such that the product becomes financially self-sustaining and competitive throughout its lifetime.

Given 13 years of hands-on operations in public and private sectors and rising to become a chief engineer, the author was faced with problems of failed and abandoned national projects in a developing country. His experience also includes over 20 years as a project management consultant in African countries representing major multinational companies; he has painfully observed the recurrent failures which are not limited to one country. Over the years, he has written more than 30 papers on project management problems in Africa. He has also spoken on the subject at international conferences in Africa.

As a result, the book will discuss the problems, suggest solutions and propose a framework that could be adapted for success by project management professionals, project owners and decision makers in their respective projects.

Target audience: The target audience or readership includes international and local persons, professionals and organisations who plan and execute projects in Africa such as:

- Consultants and contractors
- Project planners, project managers, project team members
- Maintenance and operations managers
- National and foreign governments and international organisations
- Non-governmental organisations: for-profit and not-for-profit
- Private companies and businesses
- Educational institutions and universities
- United Nations agencies
- Other professionals and professional bodies

Emphasis on competitiveness: As already stated, the main objective of this book is not just to achieve the successful delivery of projects on time and within budget but also to ensure that project deliverables are commercially and financially competitive throughout their planned lifetime. They should be planned and executed such that the deliverables, in operation, will compete successfully in the marketplace. They should earn income to pay their workers, fund their operations and maintenance, provide profits and other planned benefits for their stakeholders. The practice of funding by governments, or external organisations, of companies to ensure the survival of their project deliverables, which are produced to operate commercially, should be stopped. Companies and their deliverables should be able to survive and respond to the demands, pulls and pressures of market forces. Over the years, it is doubtful whether there have been any considerations of the return on investments in the planning and implementation of our national projects.

Our national budgets may not have been properly developed as business plans in our countries' development plans. A business plan does not just belong to the private sector. It is a plan to be used by every commercial enterprise whether government or private. The laws of market forces apply to all commercial deliverables from the public and private sectors. Therefore, if we engage in commercial enterprises in the public or private sector without due considerations of the checks and balances of market forces, we shall be penalised. The penalty could be in the form of inability to complete our projects because we have run out of money. It could also be the case that we cannot operate the commissioned deliverables because we have not provided money for them. In both cases, the projects may end up being abandoned as has been the experience with many projects in Africa over the years.

This book suggests that a project management office responsible for projects could be established with all the features and flexibilities for commercial operations. An organisation should prepare and develop its vision, mission, strategic objectives such that they should constitute the basis of the business plan which should be implemented for successful functional and commercial operations over the lifetime of the deliverables. For example, if a government or any other organisation decides to plan and implement a project such that its deliverable will operate commercially in the market, then it is imperative, for success and sustainability, that the deliverable is designed, executed and resourced to operate profitably over its planned product lifetime. It should operate independently and not depend on the government or an external organisation for its funding. This is the overarching message of this book.

Scope: The scope of the book covers investigation and discussion of the following topics:

- Causes of failure to complete projects.
- Causes of failure of the deliverables after being put into operations, making it impossible to obtain the benefits over its lifetime.
- The presentation of a framework that can be used to deliver projects such that they are completed on time and on budget, and produce deliverables which can be operated and sustained to earn income and make profits throughout their lifetime.
- Benefits management is also considered.
- Failures discussed in some industries could occur in some others. It is observed that causes of project failures are similar in many industries. For example, causes such as poor planning, lack of knowledge of project management, lack of resources, etc., run as a common thread in various industries.
- Projects discussed are those that fail during implementation or their deliverables fail soon after project completion. They may belong to the public or private sector; they may be owned by national or international organisations.
- Information from this book could prove invaluable in efforts to stop failure of projects and deliverables, whether in African countries, any developing countries, or even developed countries.
- Suggestions presented are based on principles of project management which users could adapt to their different projects, programmes and portfolios.

Structure: The book is presented as a reference book for achieving successful and sustainable project delivery in Africa, and is comprised of five sections as follows:

Section 1 comes after the Introduction, which is Chapter 1. The section is on some failed projects and project deliverables in some African countries. There is no intention to investigate failures in every country. Rather, three countries are chosen as representative of the others. These are Nigeria, Ghana and South Africa. Some failed projects in these countries are discussed in Chapters 2, 3 and 4, respectively.

In Section 2, some failed projects in some industries are considered. Again, it is not planned to discuss failed projects in all industries. Therefore, industries which are considered to be most impactful on economic development are the focus. Thus, failures in the construction industry, water projects, electricity industry, and renewable energy are discussed respectively in Chapters 5, 6, 7 and 8.

A definition of the investigated problems is considered in Section 3. Observation during research underlines the fact that causes of failures are generally not limited to given countries. Such causes of failure as poor knowledge of project management, lack of resources, corruption, etc., are not failings in just one African country. No, they occur in Nigeria, Ghana, South Africa, Kenya, etc. This knowledge informs the decision to present a chapter on definitions of the problems with examples taken from various countries. These are analysed, and suggestions made for their solutions. Therefore, problems of lack of resources, poor planning and poor project management; corruption, zero productivity and poor return on investment; and failed governance are discussed in Chapters 9, 10 and 11.

Thus far, what has been done in the chapters is a presentation of the failed projects and their causes. A piece-meal suggestion has been made for the solution of each problem. However, an objective of this book is to propose a comprehensive framework and guidelines for addressing the problems in the confidence that such an approach should prevent the occurrence of some of the problems. Besides, it will present a platform from which the problems could be effectively addressed. This is considered in Sections 4 and 5. Components of the framework, its implementation using Organisational Project Management (OPM) and Project Portfolio Management (PPM) are respective subjects of Chapters 12 and 13 in Section 4. The other components of the framework which are programme management and project management are discussed in Chapters 14 and 15. Transitioning from projects to operation is the subject of Chapter 16. In the concluding section, which is Section 5, an attempt has been made to summarise the contributions of this book by presenting its highlights and indicating where they can be found in the book. This information is presented graphically in Chapter 17, which is the last chapter. Information, consisting of explanations, some relevant extrapolations, applications and complements of the texts, etc., in the chapters has been included in the appendices.

Also included in the appendices are tested and proven project management methodologies and processes used by international organisations, companies and governments in advanced countries for preventing, amending and mitigating conditions that lead to failures of projects. An example is the use of a project management office for national project management and sustainability, such as the UK Infrastructure and Projects Authority (IPA) [9].

Following this Introduction is Section 1, which contains the description of some failed projects and project deliverables and their causes in three African countries.

Circles of causes of failures: A bold and innovative action has been taken by the introduction of Circles of Failures in this book. The objective is to present graphically on a page the various causes of failures discussed. Using this information, a researcher, a planner, a consultant or whoever needs it, can find graphically assembled on one page the various causes of failures. Therefore, the task of searching for them on various chapters and pages has been removed. The causes are assembled in the following three circles:

1. Circles of causes of project failures and abandonment in Section 3, Figure S.1.
2. Circles of corruption in project management in Chapter 10.
3. Circles of poor governance in Chapter 11.

Workshop assignments and questions: There are workshop assignments and questions at the end of each section. These are hands-on and should help the reader to understand and implement the lessons of the book.

References

1. Abimbola Ayobami, "About 12,000 federal projects abandoned across Nigeria." Retrieved November 24, 2012 from: http://saharareporters.com
2. Ayo Olukotun, "Abandoned projects and state decay," *Friday Musings*, Opinion PUNCH, Published 7 October 2016.
3. William Yaw Owusu, "STX: tale of a failed project," *General News, Daily Guide*, 10 January 2012.
4. Kemi Busari, "Investigation: the appalling, risky state of Nigeria's multi-billion Naira Nuclear Technology Centre," *Premium Times*, 21 January 2018.
5. Johnson Obera, "Governance and accountability issues in Nigerian parastatals the case of Ajaokuta steel," Doctor of Philosophy, University of Dundee, 2 February 2018.
6. Yekeen Akinwale, "The real reasons Itakpe and Ajaokuta steel companies are lying fallow," *Premium Times*, 2 February 2018.
7. Fola Ojo, "Our backyard, a giant junkyard," *Punch*, 1 September 2017.
8. Transparency International, "Global corruption barometer," 2017, http://gcb.transparency.org/
9. "IPA publishes its annual report on major projects," 19 July 2017, https://www.ukconstructionmedia.co.uk/news/ipa-publishes-annual

SECTION 1
SOME FAILED PROJECTS
AND PROJECT DELIVERABLES

This section is on some of the failed projects and project deliverables in some African countries and the causes of failures. The analysis of each example will include the following:

- A description of the failed project
- Causes of failure

The countries are Nigeria, Ghana and South Africa. Some failed projects in these countries are discussed in Chapters 2, 3 and 4 respectively. These are representative case studies. Countries and applications used here are examples as it has not been planned in this book to cover all the countries in Africa. The analysis will be sequential and conducted as follows:

- Nigeria
- Ghana
- South Africa

Accounts have been given of real-life projects, operations and failures. The objective is to present actual examples of the problems that lead to the failure of projects and project deliverables. Efforts have been made to withhold names of persons since the intention is not to embarrass individuals. Our failings and shortcomings are not and should not be blamed on individuals but on systemic failures, underdevelopment and poor project management.

Chapter 2

Examples of Failed Projects in Nigeria

As briefly stated in the introduction, a government commissioned audit revealed that 11,886 Nigerian Federal Government projects failed in 40 years up to 2011 (that is about 300 projects failed every year), with the attendant loss of billions of dollars. Reference was also made to the fact that in October 2016, a former Director-General of the Bureau of Public Procurement stated that there were 19,000 Nigerian Federal Government projects in various stages of abandonment. Some examples of major strategic industrial and scientific failed projects are examined in the next paragraphs.

Failed Nigerian Steel Industry

The iron and steel industry which was planned to be a catalyst for industrialisation failed in Nigeria for many years despite a promising start. However, between 2016 and 2019, efforts were made at reactivating some of the plants.

Initial Promising Start

Steel industrialisation was first embarked upon by the President Shehu Shagari administration between 1979 and 1983. The rolling mills were commissioned in Katsina, Oshogbo and Jos respectively. A rolling mill and a complex steel plant were also commissioned at the Delta Steel Company,

Aladja. Major construction and erection works were embarked upon at the Ajaokuta Steel Company which before it was abandoned was reportedly 98% completed. Iron-ore extraction at Itakpe was to serve as the source of raw materials for these rolling mills and the steel plants. There was a 20-year rolling plan for Nigeria's industrialisation launched by the Shagari administration in 1980. The Russians started the construction at the Ajaokuta Steel Company and these enterprises were commissioned by Shagari. There was jubilation at this significant development. In spite of this initial start, the whole programme was later abandoned for over 36 years by the intervening military governments who overthrew the government of President Shehu Shagari.

Causes of Failure

- Inability of the companies to generate fund for their operations rather depended on the Federal Government for their funding
- Failure of the government to continue to fund their operations

As the government could not continue to finance the operations of the steel plants, it privatised them. Global Steel Holding Limited (GSHL), an Indian company, reportedly acquired both Ajaokuta Steel Company Limited and Delta Steel Company Limited in 2004 and 2005 respectively from President Obasanjo "to clear the outstanding workers' salaries and take up the running of the plant." The government could not manage some of the completed plant units. It was spending a lot of money to pay salaries of hundreds of workers who were producing no income. The plants could not earn income to pay for their operations.

Disagreement over Privatisation

Ajaokuta Steel Company Limited, Nigeria Iron Ore Mining Company (NIOMCO) at Itakpe in Kogi, Delta Steel Company Limited Aladja and ALSCON, the Aluminium Smelter Company of Nigeria at Ikot-Abasi, Akwa Ibom State were some of the major steel companies privatised during the presidency of President Obasanjo. There was a serious disagreement over the privatisations such that the incoming government of President Umaru Yar'Dua did not find them acceptable and therefore nullified them. This led to years of prolonged litigation between the Nigerian Federal Government and the buyers from 2004 until 2016 when President Buhari reached an out-of-court settlement.

Reasons for the Privatisation

Poor Return on Investment, Gross Inefficiency, and Source of Major Financial Drain on the Economy

The Director-General* of the Bureau of Public Enterprises (BPE) from 1999 to 2003 explained that the government embarked on privatisation to reduce or eliminate the drain that the inefficient public enterprises constituted on the public treasury. He said that he had 33 transactions, closed 23 companies and returned N57 billion to the Federal Government treasury. He explained that from 1970 to 1999, the Federal Government invested over $100 billion in building enterprises, but earned only a 0.5% return on investment. He said that the companies were costing the government N265 billion about $1.4 billion annually to maintain. According to him

> the late 1970s was a period that public enterprises were not working instead they were not only a drain on the economy (but also) they were not providing services and not solving the problem they were meant to solve, but they were captured by the elites for their own benefits.
>
> [D]uring Abdusalami's regime, the budget of the Federal government was N300 billion, but we spent N265 billion (worth then about $2.65 billion) supporting inefficient, corrupt, and epileptic public enterprises. That was the philosophy behind privatisation and commercialisation of the companies. So, to blame privatisation for these companies not doing well is being economical with the truth.
>
> For example, Nigerian Telecommunications Limited (NITEL) for 25 years only provided 400,000 telephone lines after it had invested $7 billion for the most expensive phone system in the world, and they actually thought they were doing you a favour if they gave you a telephone line. … And to say that the purpose is to create

---

* Name withheld.

jobs is wrong. That was not the mandate to BPE, it is to remove these companies from the treasury, make them more efficient, open up the market for competition so that other operators can come in.

In the year 2000, as at December 2000, the total liabilities of 39 public enterprises was in excess of N1.1 trillion (about $11 billion) and they had accumulated losses of N92 billion naira (about $0.92 billion), and they consumed over $3 billion USD per annum or about N10 million a day. The justification for selling them was very clear and we did it. The only thing that is working in Nigeria today is what is run by private sector. Today we produced 9000 mega-watts of power in our homes with (personal and private) genera-tors while the public power supplier, NEPA, is giving us 3000.

Zero Productivity with Regular Payments on Full Salaries

Sadly, in our concept of working for the government, when one reports to the office every day, one expects to be paid, and one is not really bothered whether or not any value is generated to one's employer. The thinking is that the very act of reporting to work should attract a salary. For example, at the failed Nigeria Iron Ore Mining Company (NIOMCO), each day, a handful of the staff came around, signed their attendance register and sat in clusters for some idle chat, while some simply took a nap under trees or inside the broken-down units within the plant. They closed from their workplace when workers at other government ministries and agencies closed for the day. They generated zero income, yet they still reported to work on every work-ing day and were paid.

"That's a ritual we have been doing since this place stopped work-ing," said one of the workers, who declined to be identified because he was not allowed to talk to the press. Between 2010 and 2017, the Federal Government, according to the Budget Office of the Federation, budgeted N13.1 billion ($66 million) for the company, out of which N12.4 billion ($62million) was paid as salary. The government kept allocating budget to pay workers' salaries at Ajaokuta. In 7 years, N29.9billion was spent pay-ing workers out of the total N30.9 billion ($155 million) budgeted for both personnel and overhead for the plant. Yet the plant was not functioning, and the workers were not earning any income. In 2010 and 2011, personnel cost for the steel plant constituted the total budget for the plant: N2.3billion ($11.5 million) and N4.5billion ($22.5 million) respectively.

References 6 and 7 in Chapter 1 contain the sources of the account in this chapter.

Abandoned and Still to Be Reactivated Scientific Projects

It was on 23 December 1988 that President Ibrahim Babangida laid the foundation stone of the Sheda Science and Technology Complex (SHESTCO) at Kilometre 32, Lokoja-Abuja Road, Abuja. This was following the acceptance by the government of the recommendations of a 17-member panel of professors, doctors and technocrats who had carried out their study and deliberations for eight months. The complex was supposed to be the first-ever nuclear technology centre in Africa and to be modelled after the Tsukuba Science City in Japan, Taedok Science Town in South Korea and Serpong facility in Indonesia. It was successfully erected, and after five years, the Biotechnology, Chemistry and Physics laboratories were built.

There are four large laboratories at SHESTCO. They are the Biotechnology, Physics and Chemistry Laboratories which are in operations. The Nuclear Laboratory, which is the fourth laboratory, has not been in operation yet. Its constituent units are described in the next paragraphs, and are as follows:

1. A radioactive waste management facility
2. A nuclear instrumentation laboratory
3. Recreational and educational facility
4. A warehouse
5. An irradiation facility

1. A radioactive waste management facility

In 2009, at Nigeria's Nuclear Technology Centre (NTC), the construction of low/medium radioactive waste management facility was reportedly awarded at the contract sum of N401.4 million to Commerce General Limited. It was stated that at the time of writing in 2018 that, so far, N312 million had been paid to the contractor, as explained by the Nigeria Atomic Energy Commission (NAEC), the supposed operators of the equipment. The project, according to the NAEC, should be 78% complete. They explained that the delays were caused by "inadequate funding of capital projects generally over the years, modification of the original design, as recommended by IAEA experts, which has resulted into changes in the BOQ (bill of quantities) figures and this development is being discussed with the contractor," and also, there was "no outstanding Interim Payment Certificate on the project."

A staff member of the NTC, who had knowledge about the contract and execution since 2009, alleged corruption. He claimed that the project had been used to embezzle money from the government since the time it was awarded. He said: "It is true that they changed the plan of the plant, but they've never done anything meaningful there since they mounted these blocks. The contractor is not qualified and along the line, he got stuck in the project and we've not seen or heard about him for many years now."

According to *Premium Times* who reported this investigation, their efforts to reach the management of Commerce General Nigeria Limited, the contractors, were unsuccessful as the company had no website or any visible record. Its recorded address at Plot 3, Railway Avenue, Kachia Road, Kakuri, Kaduna South, Kaduna, did not exist.

While the commission stated the project was 78% complete, reporters claimed that a visit to the facility presented a different picture as it showed an expanse of land overgrown with weeds and construction work not half-completed. This did not justify the commission's claim of paying almost 80% of the total contract sum to the contractor. If the contract was awarded at N401.4 million ($4 million) and N312 million ($3.12 million) had been paid so far, the balance should be about N89 million but the NAEC claims that it is N329 million (about $3.29 million).

2. Abandoned nuclear instrumentation laboratory

The project for the nuclear instrumentation laboratory, which is supposed to serve as a workshop for students, researchers and others in the nuclear field, was awarded at the cost of N829.6 million (about $8.296 million) to Trois Associate Limited in 2012. It was 68% completed as the NAEC stated in a Freedom of Information request. Again, the NAEC claimed that the project was not abandoned and was delayed due to the lack of funds. "For instance, there was no provision for the project in year 2016 and only about 11% of the capital has been released so far in the current year (2017)," the response noted.

When the Premium Times representative first visited the centre in September 2017, there was no contractor on site. In fact, they reported that there was no physical way a contractor could have reached the building because there were about 100 metres of bushes and trees surrounding the laboratory building that needed to be cleared.

"The contract has been on hold due to non-payment of funds," the contractor* handling the project, told the Premium Times when contacted in October 2017.

"We demobilised in 2015 March because our outstanding valuation was not honoured by the commission. It was due payment that was just made last month." He said the project was about 75% completed as against the 68% quoted by the NAEC and that he was already on site after a recent release of fund. He would not state the amount recently released. Although the project was awarded at an agreed amount of N829.6 million (about $8.296 million), the N265.2 million (about $2.652 million) balance will not be a sufficient fund to complete the construction.

3. A recreational and educational facility

A professor[†] and the then Minister of Science and Technology, while receiving former military leader, Ibrahim Babangida, at the foundation laying ceremony of the nuclear facility in 1988, envisaged that the centre should be a "sanctuary to the scientific and technological community where members can retire to occasionally for more positive thinking about the physical."

To make that vision a reality, the Goodluck Jonathan government in 2012 made budgetary provision for the construction of a recreational and educational facility. At the time of writing, it was still abandoned, and the site was cultivated by farmers in 2018. The contract was awarded to Silhouettes AB + Turnkey at N274.5 million (about $2.74 million) and an initial payment of N214.2 million (about $2.142 million) was made, leaving a balance of N60.3 million (about $0.63 million).

Like others, construction of the sports facility was half completed and the NAEC said it was delayed due to a lack of funds. "The contractor has just been mobilised back to the site and further works on the project have commenced," the NAEC explained.

Meanwhile, staff of the NTC said they were familiar with the management's "deceptive" move of mobilising contractors back to the site whenever they sniffed a probe. "It's a game and they understand the game very well. They mobilised the same contractors back to site immediately the present administration came on board in anticipation of what may come up but

---

* Please note that the names have been omitted deliberately.
† Please note that the names have been omitted deliberately.

since there were no signs of probe everything ended that way," a staff said. The staff added that the "fire brigade approach" of mobilising contractors back to the site was only to douse the tension raised by this investigation by the *Premium Times* reporter. "They will soon abandon the project again when everything dies down," she said.

The contractor* handling the project declined to speak with Premium Times without permission from the NAEC. "Speak to NAEC and let them tell me to speak to you," he said in a phone conversation. He became agitated when reminded that the project was being funded with public money and, as such, he had a duty to answer questions relating to it.

"I'm a private man, I'm not a public man," he said angrily and hung up. It was alleged that his reluctance to speak about the project might not be unconnected with the state of the sports centre which had been turned into a farm and grazing field for farmers and cattle herders. Contrary to the claim that contractors had been mobilised, in December 2017, when the Premium Times reporter visited in January 2018, the site was still abandoned just as it was in previous visits. The only visible change was two heaps of sand delivered at the site. There was no one working there.

4. Completed – but locked – warehouse

One of the reportedly completed projects at the centre, the warehouse, had been locked since 2009 when it was completed, Premium Times learnt. According to the findings, the facility was supposed to be a warehouse for people to bring in their produce for irradiation and store the same before transporting it out of the centre. However, it was reported that none of these activities had ever happened at the centre.

"There was a time, it was thought that the Irradiation Facility could be commercialised," said the Director-General† of SHETSCO. The need for a warehouse for storing goods for irradiation was identified.

It was claimed that just before they (NAEC) left the Ministry of Science and Technology to the Presidency, someone went to the President and suggested that the facility could be commercialised. The President directed the then Minister of Science and Technology to look into the possibility.

In compliance to the directive, the Minister then set up a committee and part of the recommendation of that committee was that it could be

---

* Please note that the names have been omitted deliberately.
† Please note that the names have been omitted deliberately.

commercialised, but in the first place, a warehouse should be built. Before the report of that committee could be fully implemented, the management of the centre had gone to NAEC and NAEC had left the Ministry. However, the commercialisation has not been followed up.

5. Irradiation facility

This is one of the major facilities in the NTC. It contains a 340-kilocurie cobalt-60 irradiation source. It was inaugurated by President Obasanjo shortly before leaving office. It cost over N50 billion (about $0.5 billion) and was built for research and commercial operations, but its operation was suspect, as it had been poorly maintained since 2006.

Planned uses and applications: It was planned to be used for the peaceful application of nuclear technology in areas of agriculture, industry, health care, polymerisation, electricity generation, sterilisation, disinfection and autoradiography. Intended applications in agriculture include increased food production through the use of fast neutrons to induce mutations in seeds, sprout inhibition of onions, potatoes etc., insect disinfestations of grains, reduction in microbial load of spices, genetic engineering and breeding disease resistant plant varieties.

In addition, with a controlled injection of gamma radiation, the shelf life of perishable agricultural produce such as yam, cassava, tomatoes, beans, oranges etc. could be prolonged thereby reducing loss in the harvested foodstuffs. The potential beneficiaries are researchers, farmers, exporters and medical practitioners. Despite these huge economic potential applications, the facility was not being used because it failed to work properly.

"The facility there is already old," said the Director-General.

> We bring products in, irradiate them and take them out from the other side. But funds have not been forthcoming for us to do that the way we wanted. Since 2015, we have not seen any capital expenditure. So, this is the hard reality.

He said the facility could not irradiate up to a tonne of produce in its present condition. A nuclear technology expert and former Director* of SHETSCO noted that the facility could still be used for commercial purposes but needed to be upgraded for maximum output. He explained:

---

* Please note that the names have been omitted deliberately.

The cobalt-60 that is being used there has a half-life of about five (years). So, every five years, it deteriorates by half. It means that by 2015, it had gone down to a quarter of what it used to be. By the safety principles of International Atomic Energy Agency, IAEA, it was no longer a safe nuclear centre. Nigeria has been a member of the IAEA; we should therefore know that we are not complying by their safety standards.

He observed that the most harmful consequences arising from facilities and activities should come from the loss of control over a nuclear reactor core, nuclear chain reaction, radioactive source or other source of radiation. Consequently, to ensure that the likelihood of an accident having harmful consequences is extremely low, measures have to be taken to prevent the occurrence of failures or abnormal conditions (including breaches of security) that could lead to such a loss of control.

Investigation by Premium Times had shown that most of these breaches would have been avoided had the contracts awarded been fully executed. The mismanagement of the irradiation facility, the non-existence of a waste management facility for proper disposal of nuclear wastes and others abandoned within the centre probably should necessitate the decommissioning of the nuclear facilities.

Lack of progress: A contributory factor to this is poor decision making. As discussed earlier, the government was yet to decide on who managed the NTC and its facilities: the Ministry of Science and Technology or the Presidency. SHETSCO was under the ministry but the NTC and its facilities had been transferred to the presidency.

"Before, this centre used to be under the management of SHETSCO and things still work well, but when they transferred the management to NAEC in the Presidency, everything got destabilised." This was the testimony of one of the workers. When it was inaugurated in 2006, the Gamma facility was managed by SHETSCO who was in control of the whole complex. Three years later, in 2009, the management was transferred to the NAEC and thus, the facility and others at the NTC including the staff became the responsibility of the NAEC.

"The centre is under NAEC and NAEC receives the budget for the centre," Deputy Director,* Budget, Ministry of Science and Technology told Premium

---

* Please note that the names have been omitted deliberately.

Times during a follow-up to a Freedom of Information (FOI) request for the budget of the centre.

"SHETSCO is under the ministry and their budget is quoted in the ministry's budget. But the budget of the Nuclear Technology Centre goes directly to NAEC which is under the presidency. So, we don't have their budget here."

As reported by Premium Times, investigations revealed that the NAEC is culpable in the poor management of the Gamma facility. According to the arrangement, when the NAEC was to take over, nuclear activities at the centre including the maintenance of the Gamma facility fell under the control of the NAEC while the non-nuclear ones remained the responsibility of SHETSCO.

"Since 2009, the budget goes into NAEC," SHETSCO Director-General* said. Investigation by the Premium Times reveals that the budgetary provision for the centre to the NAEC is about N13 billion ($0.13 billion) for personnel, recurrent and capital expenditure for the commission in the past five years.

Inadequate funding: As already reported, the chairman† of the NAEC defended the commission, saying it was hampered by inadequate funding. While admitting that the facility was not properly maintained, he explained:

> There is nothing like NTC budget fundamentally, what we do (is that) government funds projects and they allocate funds (to) the project. On the recurrent, even under SHETSCO, the NTC never had a separate budget, it was SHETSCO budget. Somehow, we have a one-line budget without specifying which centre has what.
>
> For instance, our overhead cost (received) in the last two, three years is less than N12 million ($0.12 million) monthly, for all the headquarters and all these centres, you have to manage it. Last year we had an overhead of only 8 months, this year we have had only six months. So, there is no magic we can do.

Why Was the Centre Not Completed?

The reasons, which were the causes of failure, include the following:

---

* Please note that the names have been omitted deliberately.
† Please note that the names have been omitted deliberately.

Ill-Defined Responsibilities for Management of the NTC

The Nuclear Technology Centre (NTC) was initially a unit in Sheda Science and Technology Complex (SHETSCO), which was in the Ministry of Science and Technology until 2009. It was then transferred to the Nigeria Atomic Energy Commission (NAEC), which was a department in the presidency. However, this transfer had not been fully implemented and this contributed to the failures in the management of the operations of some of the units of NTC such as the Nuclear Instrumentation Laboratory and others.

Idleness at Work, Zero Productivity

There had been a drastic non-availability of tools to work with, such that some staff of the centre informed the reporting investigator that they came to work daily to do nothing as the machines were no longer working. One of them explained that the situation was better when the centre was run solely by SHETSCO. She said:

It's not only about salary but I also have to think about my career. Even though my salary is being paid regularly but I've not been doing anything for years now. Nothing is working here, and we can't continue to keep quiet. We come here every day just to talk and while away time. Nothing is functioning here.

Another staff said that he was unhappy at being idle and urged the government to merge the nuclear centres into one entity. He explained:

It's better that the place is left to be managed by one entity. If there is any fault now, you will see that there will be shift of blame. So, let everything that happens here be on one person. We don't want SHETSO, NAEC joint management again. We want just one. We want to work.

Fund Limitation

The Chairman* of NAEC explained:

If you've not been able to secure funds, irrespective of who is managing it, you will not be able to do anything. For instance, if a facility develops some fault and to fix that somebody gives you

---

* Please note that the names have been omitted deliberately.

about €800 bill, you have to plan that in the budget before you could get it repaired. But what we have challenged our staff to do is that there are some of those things they can work on themselves. So, it's not a question of people go there and no work, but the challenges of fund and we are working to get appropriate funding. With the support we are gradually getting from the government, we are likely going to solve some of those problems within the next year.

Going Forward: Road Map

The Federal Government in August 2017 approved a 13-year National Science, Technology and Innovation Road Map, starting from 2017 to 2030. The minister* of Science and Technology, in 2018, stated at the presentation of the South-West Sensitization Programme on National Science, Technology and Innovation Roadmap, that the roadmap should save the country about $11 billion in five years. He said the roadmap should enhance the nation's emerging post-crude oil economy, catalyse economic growth and boost competitiveness of the nation's raw material endowment.

A former Director-General† of the nuclear centre said: "It is unfortunate that we keep talking about nuclear programme, but the government is not spending on this." He continued:

> Any programme that will gulp money, the government can propagate it but later turn their eye to it and nuclear technology is always expensive to run. They need to put more money. For example, nuclear technology can be used in power generation. We can ask our friends in other parts of the world to come and invest in nuclear technology but first, we must put our money down. It is business. We can get up to 5,000 megawatts from a nuclear source in the next five years if we take deliberate steps. We can target.

In the meantime, the centre remained abandoned and was in urgent need of reactivation.

---

* Please note that the names have been omitted deliberately.
† Please note that the names have been omitted deliberately.

Observations and Comments

While workers accuse their management of corruption and mismanagement of funds, the management responded that it was a case of inadequate fund for their operations. Moreover, no fund was specifically allocated for running any facility.

The failure to complete the infrastructure of these strategic scientific facilities could be attributed to poor project management and failure of subsequent governments to provide adequate resources. It appeared that the individual users were left to manage them, and the accountability had been poor.

Setting up such strategic and expensive projects without any reliable central project management team to supervise gave way to abuse and allegations of corruption, mismanagement of funds and failures. The vision and objectives became lost in the morass of everyday commonplace mismanagement of fund that is a feature of government projects in Africa. A former country's vice president* had said a project belonging to everybody belongs to nobody. This statement seems to be borne out by the corruption and mismanagement of public fund observed in these projects. The sad accounts of the huge losses sustained in the uncompleted and practically abandoned facilities after much money had been sunk into their projects greatly underscore the need for a national project management unit that should be responsible for such major strategic projects to prevent such unbridled waste and continuing drain of scarce national resources.

Nigeria Is the Largest Importer of Petrol Because of Non-Functional Refineries [1]

Speaking on 1 March 2018, Group Managing Director (GMD)† of the Nigerian National Petroleum Corporation (NNPC) stated that Nigeria was the only member country in the Organisation of Petroleum Exporting Countries (OPEC) that imported petrol, that is Premium Motor Spirit (PMS), and was currently the largest importer in the world. The GMD was represented by the Chief Operating Officer (COO),‡ Upstream, who made this statement at

---

* Please note that the names have been omitted deliberately.
† Names omitted deliberately
‡ Names omitted deliberately

the 2018 Oloibiri Lecture Series. He described as "shameful" the situation where Nigeria, Africa's top oil producer, depended on petrol imports to meet daily needs.

Causes of the failure: In this period which included 2018, Nigeria had four refineries located in Port Harcourt (two), Warri and Kaduna, with combined installed capacity to refine 445,000 barrels of crude per day but these had not been working properly for years. This was allegedly because top oil industry officials and politicians reportedly diverted huge funds earmarked for their routine comprehensive turnaround maintenance. It was feared that the four refineries had not undergone comprehensive repairs in a decade or more as contracts awarded for their repairs were either abandoned halfway or not executed at all.

Comments

It is instructive that it was the Group Managing Director of NNPC who described as shameful our failure to refine our crude locally to produce our own petrol requirements. This statement is suggestive and probably indicative of the fact that he did not find himself or his corporation liable for the failure. On the face of it, one would think that it was their responsibility, but he appeared to disown it. Invariably, the Federal Government appeared to be implicated.

A message one could take away from this event is the possibility that the Federal Government had not given them a free hand to operate and discharge their responsibilities as best as they would want to do.

Little or No Accountability and "White Elephant Projects" [2]

It had been the practice for many years, especially since after the Nigerian Civil War, from 1971 to 2019 – the timing of the writing of this book – that state governors, federal ministers, whether military or civilian, etc., had managed their ministries, and projects with little or no accountability. Each managed their areas of responsibilities as their personal estates. A Bureau of Public Procurement was established in 2007 but it is doubtful how much control that this organisation has exerted, over the years, on the heads of the Nigerian federal and state government – these are the presidents, governors and ministers, in their engagement in projects on behalf of the country with foreign companies. Nigerian governors and presidents, at the time of writing and for some years before, had immunity from prosecution while in office. However, directly they completed their terms of office, many of them faced investigation and prosecution for mismanagement of fund and money laundering. This happened especially to persons whose party was no longer in power. They were sadly covered if their party was still in charge of the Federal Government. Some of these projects have resulted in white elephant projects; these are discussed in the next paragraphs. A white elephant project is one which is expensive to maintain or difficult to dispose of because the cost of making, keeping or maintaining it is far higher than its usefulness or value.

Questionable and "White Elephant" Projects in Nigeria [2] and Other African Countries

It had been said that public office holders who embarked on such white elephant projects were motivated by the desire to impress the public in the knowledge that most Nigerians hardly bothered to explore the economic justification of government projects. Moreover, such projects, whose costs were allegedly often inflated, provided avenues through which public funds were reportedly "siphoned" or secreted away.

An example was that some 100 students, from Kano State, were sent in March 2013 to undergo an 18-month professional pilot training course at the Mid-East Aviation Academy, Amman, Jordan, at the cost of $6.7 million [3]. A report in the *Daily Trust* (newspaper) of 1 March 2016 referred to the *Daily Trust* on Sunday the week before that 100 promising young men and women that were sent abroad by a state government to undergo training as commercial pilots ended up as civil servants and classroom teachers on their return. An investigation in February 2016 by the *Daily Trust*, found that there were already about 600 qualified but unemployed pilots in the country. It also reported that about 80 of them had come back to the country following their graduation; however, some of them had been employed by the state government as regular civil servants, some of whom were classroom teachers.

In the same vein, a former state governor also sponsored some 25 students from Kano state for a 4-year course in Marine Engineering in the United States and India at a staggering cost of $80 million per annum, (i.e. $320 million for the 4 years) according to the Director of Press to Governor.

Kano is a geographically landlocked state in Northern Nigeria, there are no rivers or boats and ships to provide suitable job opportunities for the students when they graduate.

Causes of Failure

Failure to have carried out appropriate feasibility studies before embarking on these "white elephant" projects accounts for their failure. These examples highlight and demonstrate the poor accountability and absence of supervision to justify investments on such projects. Therefore, poor governance, poor accountability and control and questionable use of public funds, which engender corruption, are some of the reasons for the existence of failed projects in the form of "white elephant" projects which are hardly any good to the public.

Failure to Plan for Sustainability of Projects and Project Deliverables

The effect of failure to plan for sustainability of projects and project deliverables is discussed in the next paragraph as it is one of the factors that turned Nigeria into a leading nation in failed projects.

Various Nigerian governments over the years have imported modern equipment and facilities into our country which has a developing economy with a comparatively poor and underdeveloped intrinsic industrial base. In the past 60 or more years, projects of the then ultra-modern power stations and steel plants, among other industrial facilities, had been implemented, commissioned and put into operations.

Following the failure of parts which could not be procured, especially plant electronics, control and automation systems and equipment, it became impossible to keep some production and ancillary plants in operation. This contributed to the abandonment of many commissioned industrial plants just three to four years after being commissioned into operation.

Personal Experience: Failure of Delta Steel Company

It is counterproductive, ill-advised and indeed a questionable use of national resources for a nation to keep importing equipment without any guarantee of their long-term sustainability. This writer finds this project procurement practice reprehensible because of the bad experiences which he personally had in working on projects in our Federal Government owned companies. As the Head of Control, Instrumentation and Computer Systems Department, he had the responsibility for engineering management of automation systems in the Delta Steel Company Limited, Aladja, Warri, Nigeria. Therefore, he had a first-hand experience of the problems created when projects that cannot be sustained and supported through their planned lifetime are imported and implemented in the country. They fail in a few years and become abandoned. The costly and magnificent Delta Steel Complex, which was reportedly built at a cost of $1.2 billion, had been abandoned because of the unsustainable costs of keeping it in operation. In this case, it was not just maintenance costs but also poor and inadequate generation of income. As we read in the earlier sections, the federal government was constrained to privatise it and it did not fare any better with the new managers. It was abandoned for years before being acquired by new owners who are trying to restore it to production at this time of writing in 2018 and 2019.

Absence of Project Management Office: International Practice for National Project Management and Sustainability

In some developed countries, there are national and government project management offices and agencies staffed with appropriate professionals with expertise in various technical specialities who have responsibilities for both short and long-term national projects. Such professionals participate in project negotiation. They also plan for the long-term sustainability of major projects in the nation. In the UK for example, there is the Infrastructure and Projects Authority (IPA). Statistics given which show information on the performance of respective national project management in Nigeria and the UK hardly bear any close comparison. In our case, losses running into billions of Naira from abandoned projects are discussed. While in the UK, 60% success is being estimated for the 2016–2017 period. Our statistics for this period may or may not exist. It is in our interest that we learn from the UK and other developed countries how they plan, invest and operate their programmes and portfolios of projects successfully.

Going Forward

Necessity for a Nigerian National Project Management Office

The UK Infrastructure and Projects Authority (IPA) is described as a unit which "works across government to support the successful delivery of all types of infrastructure and major projects; ranging from railways, schools, hospitals and housing, to IT, defence, and major transformation programmes."

This underscores the fact that, for success and sustainability of projects, we need professionals with expertise in relevant technical specialities. The way forward should be to establish them as a unit, a National Project Management Office (NPMO), charged with the responsibility of end-to-end project management in the country. The National Assembly should empower the NPMO to participate with government departments and ministries in discussion and investments in future major projects. No ministry should procure projects for the country independently. It has been shown in this book with the example on "white elephant projects" that the Nigerian Bureau of Public Procurement, the regulatory authority responsible for the monitoring and oversight of public procurement, had hardly any control on major project procurements in the country by state governors and federal ministers.

Questions

1. Why did the steel companies fail?
2. Do you know of other companies which depend on government funding for their operations? Can you dispassionately discuss their performance?
3. Can you cite instances in the chapter where work was delayed because of no funding from the government?
4. These clearly demonstrate that complete dependence on the government should not be encouraged. Each organisation should earn an income for its operations. How can these be achieved?
5. Please note that the failures presented in this section involved all the parties whether public or private sector workers. Should you encourage such an arrangement? Do you know of any such companies which have failed or are operating successfully?
   – What is a "white elephant" project?

- Why could it occur in a country?
- What could be the necessities of a national project management unit?
- Are there any failures in project delivery in your country which could have been checked and stopped by a national project management unit?

References

1. "Outrageous lies about Nigeria's refineries" Posted by: mms plus in NEWS LENS, OIL & GAS 3 July 2018, https://mmsplusng.com/blog/outrageous-lies-about-nigerias-refineries/
2. Mohammad Qaddam Sidq Isa, "Nigeria: white elephant projects," *Daily Trust* (Abuja), 25 February 2016.
3. Joy Ogbebo, "Pilots now teachers in Kano," *Category: News,* 1 March 16, Mamaj's Aviation Blog; http://mamajsaviationblog.com/2016/03/4854/

Chapter 3

Examples of Failed Projects in Ghana

In this chapter, some failures in Ghana will be presented. The objective is to show real-life examples of failures in our project delivery. As much as possible, names of persons will not be given. Similar failures also occur in Nigeria, other African countries and probably other countries.

Failure of the Ghana-STX Building Project: A $10 Billion Housing Project [1]

Many Ghanaians were shocked when they heard on 30 December 2011 about the failure and abandonment of the $10-billion housing project between the Government of Ghana and STX Engineering & Construction Limited of South Korea.

The project consisted of the construction of 200,000 houses in Ghana in five years. The agreement was signed in 2009 and hailed by some as "the best thing ever to happen to Ghana." A 12-member government delegation led by the then Minister of Water Resources Works and Housing signed the STX Housing Project deal in 2009. President Mills was quoted as saying at the sod cutting ceremony that the STX Housing Project was tied to the ruling party's 2008 manifesto commitment to expand infrastructure. He said:

> This is a significant turning point in the history of our dear country. This is the change we promised, and the government intends

to leave a strong and positive legacy and the completion of this project will be a legacy that history will not be able to write.

In August 2010, the parliament approved an initial off-take agreement for 30,000 housing units for the security agencies at a proportionate cost of $1.5 billion amid protest from the opposition New Patriotic Party (NPP).

Failure: Information on its failure and abandonment was disclosed on Friday, 30 December 2011, by Vice President John Dramani Mahama in the National Democratic Congress (NDC) government when he talked with the Parliamentary Press Corp in Accra.

Causes of failure: From research findings, causes of failure include the following:

■ **Absence of the effective management of the project by the Ghanaian Government:** Effective governance apparently was missing as disunity and quarrels were reported between the Ghanaian and Korean partners of STX Engineering & Construction Ghana Limited, the local subsidiary of STX Korea.

■ **Corruption:** This was probably a contributory factor. For example, the consulting architectural concept design allegedly prepared by a professor* at the Kwame Nkrumah University of Science and Technology (KNUST), on the orders of the CEO[†] of STX Engineering & Construction Ghana Limited, the local subsidiary of STX Korea, cost the company about $21 million, while the Koreans claimed they could do it for only $5 million.

■ **Others:** Other causes included poor planning and the absence of credible feasibility studies.

More causes of failure of other projects in Ghana include the following [2]:

Lack of accountability: There were instances where a state official chaired a government project and also was the sole contractor and supplier of materials for the same project. Rates used in the project were above the prevailing market rate (Takyi-Boadu, 2011; Ghanaweb, 2011; Ghanaian Chronicle, 2012). It was also reported that in some cases, the supplier of materials for the projects could be the same government official who awarded the contract. In effect, the government official awarded the contract

---

* Names deliberately omitted.
[†] Names deliberately omitted.

to himself, or colluded with the supplier to inflate the prices and they shared the excess as "profits."

Delay in payment: Another source of corruption arose from the failure to pay contractors in time and as due. There had been much bureaucratic procedure in government project implementation and the numerous unnecessary channels for the government project contractors to go through to obtain their payment. In order to cut down on the delay, they did a "follow-up" by making payments or bribes to relevant government officials to "speed up the payment" process. In effect, the slow pace of the payment process constrained contractors to pay bribes in return for due payment.

10% payment: Of the contractor respondents of a survey conducted by a PhD student in Ghana (referenced), 70% reported the payment of 10% of the contract money to government officials. They alleged that it was "extremely difficult or impossible" for a contractor to win a contract if the money was not paid.

Unofficial middlemen: It was reported that there were "unofficial and unauthorised middlemen" between government officials and contractors during the award of contracts. They served as the "link" between the contractor and the public servant. It was alleged that "rarely will you be able to win a contract if you do not have such middlemen who can connect you." These middlemen became influential because government officials used them as fronts. As a result, they charged both the contractor and the government officials for their services. These charges were added onto the contract sum. They linked the contractors with the government officials to make a deal. The deal could be such that sometimes the contracts were awarded to the contractors even before the official bidding took place. In that case, the official contract bidding was just a "window dressing" as the winner had already been chosen through the unofficial deal.

The other damage done by this corrupt practice was that the relevant government officials were unable to supervise the project effectively and to enforce high quality of work to ensure compliance with work specifications. Moreover, contracts were often awarded to family and political party members. Profits from contracts awarded to party members were sometimes ploughed back to party funds.

Poor planning: This manifested in the following ways:

- **Starting more projects than the organisation could finance:** The reason was that they failed to carry out proper budget planning on the number and costs of projects that could be financed. They engaged in too many projects to fulfil unrealistic campaign promises which could not be funded.

■ Sometimes they started a number of projects at the same time in order to please all the communities even if they could not be funded.

Incompetent leadership: Some project leaders without any project knowledge were appointed on the basis of political patronage rather than competence. Others assumed leadership position because of their position in the company or institution in spite of their lack of knowledge of project management. As a result, they could not plan or direct the project properly.

Uncommitted government officers: It was alleged that officers from government Ministries, Departments and Agencies (MDAs) were not dedicated to projects and were not interested in them. As a result, the project documents could be abandoned on a table for months without being attended to.

Refusal to monitor and inspect project and project abandonment: It was reported that government consultants often failed to turn up to inspect projects as expected. To resolve this, contractors were compelled to bribe them by paying for their unofficial "fuel costs" so that they agreed to visit the project site for inspection. Contractors did this because without such inspections, the projects might not continue. It was also reported that if the contractors refused, the project leaders would do everything possible to make the projects fail. For example, they would not approve documentation for such contractors. One contractor reported that when he refused to pay for the fuel of a government officer, the officer refused to sign his documents. As he waited and saw that his documents could not be signed, he also abandoned the project, and it remained abandoned even at the time he was interviewed.

Cultural misinformation of government tasks and projects as "national cake": There was the unfortunate cultural misinformation that money belonging to the nation was a "national cake." Therefore, doing a project or an assignment for the government provided one with the opportunity to cut as much as possible from the cake. This also encouraged embezzlement not only in Ghana but also in Nigeria, and probably in other African countries.

Lack of capacity: This was the unavailability of the required machinery and materials to carry out projects. Sometimes, some contractors borrowed from others when working on government projects.

Poor financial management: Often, the payment was not made as agreed on donor agencies funds. Sometimes, the money was diverted to projects for which they were not provided.

Lack of continuity: The lack of continuity of projects by political leaders affected the success of Ghanaian government projects. It was observed that when another government, especially from a different party, came into power, it decided to abandon the project. The reason was mostly political because it wanted to achieve the party's manifesto promise. It would not want to go ahead with any projects that promoted the interests of its opponents; rather, it would abandon such projects and start its own. This was irrespective of the huge financial loss this action could cause the country. This also had been happening in Nigeria and accounted for a number of abandoned projects.

An effective national project management office should stop such practices and ensure that projects undertaken are continued to meet the national strategic interests of the country irrespective of who started them.

Poor communication: Some politicians implemented projects in fulfilment of campaign promises instead of projects requested by the community. It was alleged that a community local government failed to find out why members of the community were contracting a disease but assumed that providing a water borehole should help stop the disease. However, the people refused to use the provided borehole because of their traditional belief in the use of water from the stream.

Suggestions for success in Ghana:

- As suggested for Nigeria, the Ghanaian government should institute national project management offices which should be separate from government agencies. This institution should help reduce political interference and political patronage that engender corruption.
- Laws should be passed by the parliament that projects should not be halted when there was a change of government.
- A national development project management unit to set out projects and programmes for development devoid of politics should be established.

Questions

- What are the causes of project failures discussed in this chapter?
- What are reasons for the existence of the causes?

- How can those causes be eliminated?
- Now that you are aware of those causes, how can you avoid and prevent them?

References

1. O. Chima Okereke, "Causes of failure and abandonment of projects and project deliverables in Africa," *PM World Journal*, Vol. VI, No. I, January 2017, www.pmworldjournal.net Featured Paper.
2. I. S. Damoh, "An investigation into the causes and effects of project failure in government projects in developing countries: Ghana as a case study," A thesis submitted in partial fulfilment of the requirements of Liverpool John Moores University for the degree of Doctor of Philosophy, October 2015.

Chapter 4

Examples of Failed Projects in South Africa

Our research reveals two almost diametrically opposite descriptions of performance in project delivery in South Africa. The first is a description of failure and its characteristics. The second is a number of accounts of success in current project delivery. It appears that there has been much improvement on their earlier failures. For completeness, descriptions of the two performances are discussed starting with an article entitled: "South Africa: Why Have All the Rural Tech Projects Failed?" by Kathryn Cave, Editor at IDG Connect dated 21 June 2013 [1]. We shall discuss the reported reasons for the failure and also other failed projects. According to her, poor planning and implementation, as described below, was the main reason.

Poor Planning and Implementation: Poor Project Management

The author reported scepticism in the planning and implementation of major projects. Quoting Schofield, she wrote:

> Nearly every government plan talks about what will be achieved at the end of 10, 20, 40 years – none of them is held to account for steps along the way. [South Africa is] small on delivery, poor at executing the plans, lousy at monitoring progress and ironing out the problems that arise along the way.

This summarised the views of the then Vice Chairman* of Africa ICT Alliance (Africa Information & Communication Technologies Alliance). His comments were made on the National ICT Plan and the Universal Service and Access Agency (USAASA). The aim of the plan was described as follows: "This state-owned entity of government aims to ensure that every man, woman and child whether living in the remote areas of the Kalahari or in urban areas of Gauteng will be able to connect, speak, explore and study using ICT." He commented that the organisation was "sitting on billions of Rands that it does not know how to spend ... and what has been spent has achieved little."

Other failures: They include the following:

Nelson Mandela Bay Metropolitan Municipality Metro Buses: A Failed but Not Abandoned Project [2]

Organization: Nelson Mandela Bay Metropolitan Municipality (NMBMM) – South Africa

Project type: Metro bus purchase

Project name: Integrated Public Transport System (IPTS)

Date: February 2015

Cost: R2 billion ZAR (approximately $130 million)

Synopsis: Sixty buses purchased at a cost of R100 million (ZAR) in 2009 have turned to a failed project. They were purchased as part of a programme to refresh municipal bus service in Port Elizabeth, South Africa. They were used during the 2010 Soccer World Cup but up to 2018 they were still parked.

The bus purchase was part of a larger R2 billion ($130 million) project to implement a Bus Rapid Transit system in Port Elizabeth, which started in 2008. Sadly, they are yet to be used in operation.

Causes of failure: The problems identified are as follows:

- The specification was wrong, and this resulted in the purchase of buses that are too large for the driving lanes.
- There was a failure to identify the need to drop passengers off on "central islands," which resulted in the doors ending up on the wrong side of the bus.

---

* Name omitted deliberately.

Project failed but not abandoned: It was reported that from 2008 to 2013 the project had been through five different engineering companies and four project managers. Whilst this was worrying, it was better that efforts were being made to resolve the issues than the project being abandoned as it could happen in some other African countries.

Contributing factors to project failure included:

- Poor requirements management
- Lack of attention to detail (resulting in faulty requirements)
- Dysfunctional decision making
- Failure to engage stakeholders
- High staff turnover levels

Failure in the Telecommunications Industry in South Africa [3]

Sentech was the first company in South Africa to launch a wireless broadband service, introducing services in the 3.5GHz band under the brand MyWireless in 2002. However, due to poor financial operations there was only a limited rollout to parts of Johannesburg, Cape Town, Durban, Pretoria and Nelspruit. It was eventually abandoned.

Causes of failure of the Sentech's MyWireless in South Africa:

- **Poor financial management:** In October 2010, Sentech could not collect more than 60% of the money that it was owed. Its former leadership went aground amidst accusations of mismanagement, and the auditor-general was concerned they could not pay their bills to creditors.
- **Poor business management:** The MyWireless product was terminated in 2009 after the company proved it was unable to compete with better-resourced private-sector operators in the retail consumer market. To worsen the situation, Sentech could not organise itself to make a presentation to parliament's portfolio committee on communications.

Comments: It is relevant to observe that in spite of the failures they experienced, Sentech Limited had been reorganised to a successful State-Owned Enterprise (SOE) operating in the broadcasting signal distribution and telecommunications sectors and reporting to the Minister of Telecommunication and Postal Services. Probably, one of the positive lessons that could be taken away from the story of Sentech is that in spite of a temporary failure, an African company, like a company in developed countries, could be turned around if it was reorganised with changes in its management and if it was properly funded from the start before being left to operate independently.

Microsoft's Digital Villages in South Africa [4]

Genesis and importance: On 9 March 1997, Bill Gates reportedly launched the "Digital Villages" concept in the black township of Soweto, which had made headline news by its mass uprising in 1977. This township suffered and probably still suffers from extreme poverty. It was reported in the *Spokesman-Review*, a daily newspaper in Spokane, Washington, USA, that when Gates visited in 1997, "a computer could cost as much as a house" and few people would think of going online.

The centre launched was South Africa's first free access "Digital Village," funded by Microsoft, local computer companies and US development organisation, Africare. The concept was that the $100,000 computer package, housed in the Chiawelo Community Centre, should give the township's poor residents a link to the information age. As part of the opening, Gates observed a class from the local Elsie Ngidi primary school using computers for the first time, before reportedly telling a crowd of 200: "Soweto is a milestone. There are major decisions ahead about whether technology will leave the developing world behind. This is to close the gap."

Failed and abandoned project, or was it? It was reported that even by 2013, there was hardly any evidence of the "Digital Villages" across South Africa. "[They] worked well for a while but collapsed as soon as the sponsors stopped funding the activities – the community had failed to make the use of technology self-sustaining." A one-time Vice Chairman of Africa ICT Alliance, Adrian Schofield, explained: "What should have been a model for others to follow became a failure. This is a common outcome, where there is no long-term follow through" [4].

Digital Villages resuscitated? However, the report of the complete collapse of the concept in all of South Africa appears not well founded. It was likely that the computer package, housed in the Chiawelo Community Centre, might have failed but there were other Digital Villages, based on the concept, in other areas of South Africa. Some of these are discussed in the next paragraphs.

Equipping Rustenburg schools with technology – Digital Village:
Microsoft, Comparex Africa, Anglo Platinum, Telkom Foundation and the
Digital Partnership joined forces through the Kopano Joint Venture to
equip three Rustenburg schools with technology. The computer centres
were officially opened and handed over to the school communities by
Andile Ngcaba, the Director-General, Department of Communications during a ceremony at Sedibelo Middle School in Moruleng, Rustenburg, on
23 May 2003.

Lessons from the organisation of the "Digital Villages" concept:
Microsoft presented the following business plan and guideline for how
the company implemented the establishment of "Digital Villages" in South
Africa. This has been adapted and modified for this publication.

Aims and strategy: When a suitable centre has been identified, the
community will be engaged in negotiations and discussions on the project.
The following actions should be taken:

- A committee comprising the partners and the community is established.
- The community members are trained and prepared for the takeover
  once they are ready and the business partners have completed their
  term as per agreement.
- An agreement is drafted to specify the roles and responsibilities of the
  business partners and the community members. This is done to define
  the relationship to prevent any misunderstanding.
- Funding of the Digital Village, in both the present and future, is discussed and planned.
- Microsoft approaches its business partners to donate hardware. Joint
  venture programmes are encouraged to ensure that hardware is available for the project.

Other joint venture initiatives cover administrative costs, training and the
future planning for the centre.

Project sustainability: To ensure sustainability of the project, the
following actions are embarked upon:

- Training: As already stated, the established committee members are
  trained and assisted to prepare for the self-maintenance and operation
  of the centre.
- The students are encouraged to form computer clubs and contribute
  towards the usage of the centre.

- Adults are expected to contribute a minimal sum of money to be registered as members of the centre.
- The committee is assisted to open a bank account where these contributions will be deposited.
- A Trust Fund will be established to allow the committee to raise funds on behalf of the centre.
- The viability of a particular centre will be evaluated on an agreed and regular basis and will be subject to the continued interest of all parties.

Evaluation and measurement of success: They are as follows:

- Annual evaluation is conducted, and recommendations are made for further improvement of the centres. Relevant stakeholders will be identified, and participation is invited where applicable.
- The project is considered successful in communities where evidence of commitment, achievement, organisation and structure is present.
- The support of the community is assessed through the number of paid-up memberships, the number of regular attendees and the trainees per courses offered at the centre.

Comments

The Microsoft-operated Digital Villages concept is a classic illustration of planning a project, properly resourcing it and providing resources for its follow-up when it goes into operation. This is followed by regular monitoring of its performance to ensure that the project deliverables do not fail. It could be a model to be adapted according to local requirements in providing foreign aided services to the developing world. The concept espoused in the Digital Villages programme exemplifies the suggestions being made in this book on how to achieve success and sustainability of projects and project deliverables.

Questions

1. List the failed projects and reasons for their failures.
2. How could the failures be avoided in similar projects in the future?
3. What accounted for the success of Digital Villages?
4. What could be learnt from them in setting up?

References

1. Kathryn Cave, "South Africa: why have all the rural tech projects failed?" IDG Connect, 21 June 2013.
2. Afikile Lagunya, "Nelson Mandela Bay IPTS buses to finally hit the road end of October," 4 October 2017, https://www.rnews.co.za/article/nelson-mandela-bay-ipts-buses-to-finally-hit-the-road-end-of-october
3. Rudolph Muller, "Failed telecoms projects in SA," *Mybroadband*, TechCentral, 28 March 2011.
4. "Microsoft digital villages," https://www.microsoft.com/southafrica/community/digital.htm

SECTION 2
FAILURES IN SOME INDUSTRIES

In this section, project failures in some industries are examined. These are representative of failures in most industries in Africa. The causes of failures and lessons that could be learnt to prevent reoccurrence should be some of the takeaway points from this section.

Failed Projects in Some Industries in Africa

- Some failures in construction industry
- Some failures in completed water projects in Africa
- Some failures in power supply
- Some failures in renewable energy projects

Chapter 5

Failures in Construction Industry

The construction industry has been identified as the most corrupt sector in the world. Transparency International describes construction as an industry with characteristics that render it prone to corruption. Some of the corrupt practices presented in Ghana were from the construction industry. Questionable practices in some other countries, including those outside Africa, are summarised in this chapter. This is an acknowledgement that much information in this chapter has been adapted from a paper, as referenced, written by Paul Bowen, Keith Cattell and Peter Edwards [1]. The internal references have also been culled from their material.

Australia: May et al. examined bid-cutting in construction tendering in Queensland from economic, legal, ethical and management perspectives. It was found that, after their tender had been successful, main contractors coerced subcontractors into reducing the subcontract prices used to support the original bid.

United States: Fails Management Institute/Construction Management Association of America (FMI/CMAA) found that 84% of the building owners, architects, building services firms, construction managers, contractors and subcontractors, who responded to a survey, had been exposed to construction industry-related acts or transactions that they would consider unethical.

UK: The Chartered Institute of Building (CIOB, 2006), in its survey on corruption in the UK construction industry, reported that a small majority of respondents in the study experienced corruption in the industry [2].

China: The corrupt practices in Chinese construction industry included administrative interference, the illegal award of contracts or subcontracts, the disclosure of confidential information to certain tenderers and the extortion of kickbacks by clients and government officials from contractors. Contractor-centred corruption was found to comprise the offering of bribes (money or benefits in kind) to clients or tender committee members in an endeavour to secure a tender, collusive tendering and bid rigging; invoice fraud; the use of sub-standard materials and workmanship; and collusion between contractors and supervisory authorities.

South Africa: Information from a paper, adapted as referenced, which was written by Paul Bowen, Keith Cattell and Peter Edwards [1], is still used here. They conducted a survey and obtained the results discussed in the following section. Overall, 71% of all respondents reported that they considered corruption to be widespread. Verbatim responses from some of them included statements and answers such as:

> If you do not engage in the bribery, you will either not get the job, or you will bump into various obstacles that will prevent you from doing your work as required.

> It is easier to follow the pack than stand against corruption.

> Corruption in the construction industry is rife, perpetuated mainly by government officials for personal or political gain.

> When I tender as a consulting engineer, I am almost always phoned by public officials for kickbacks, bribes, etc., sometimes during the tender stage, most of the time before they want to award the tender.

> It is during the tender and evaluation phase where generally corrupt officials within the client bodies can manipulate tenders and tender results to suit their own purposes. This is where some tenders are deemed non-responsive and ineligible based on insignificant reasons to elevate favoured tenderers.

It was generally observed across all respondent groups that government officials, who were the clients, were most frequently involved in corruption compared to the other respondent groups. Contractors were observed to be the next most corrupt group, followed by subcontractors and building inspectors. Engineers, architects and quantity surveyors were reportedly the least corrupt groups of professionals. More statements from the respondents included the following:

> Local Authorities have fine-tuned their corrupt practices. They promise all tenderers that they are going to influence the award of tenders and then extort kickbacks from the successful bidder. There is no apparent paper trail.

> It is standard industry practice that one is obliged to pay public officials for work, pay for processing of payments, pay for meetings. This payment process starts at the top of most organizations and the amounts decrease in descending positions of the individuals.

> Public officials deliberately overpay favoured contractors irrespective of the official payment certificate.

> I was told by a contractor how they manipulated tender prices as far back as 1983/84 (this was some 30 years earlier).

> Kickback to monitoring and evaluation (M&E) consultants is becoming an increasing problem.

At least 77% of all respondents agree about these concerns. Other factors revealed in statements include the following which have been adapted in this report:

- There is poor project planning on government projects. For example, close out reports on government projects hardly exist.
- There are poor skills which show up as poor financial management and lack of auditing procedures. The latter provides ample opportunity for bribery, theft and fraud.
- It is suspected that there could be the absence of political will to tackle corruption in South Africa; this makes it difficult to find discipline in its construction sector [1].

Questions

1. Some real-life testimonies have been presented in this chapter. What are they? How can the listed faults be eliminated?

2. One of the reasons for presenting these cases is to inform anyone who wishes to do business that such problems exist. How can you prepare your team not to fall prey to them?

References

1. P. Bowen, P. Edwards and K. Cattell, "Corruption in the South African construction industry: a mixed methods study," Smith, S.D (Ed), Procs 28th Annual ARCOM Conference, 3–5 September 2012, Edinburgh, UK, Association of Researchers in Construction Management, pages 521–531. http://www.arcom.ac.uk/-docs/proceedings/ar2012-0521-0531_Bowen_Edwards_Cattell.pdf
2. Fiona Campbell, "Corruption in the UK Construction Industry 2006," The Chartered Institute of Building, 10 January 2006.

Chapter 6

Failures in Water (Borehole) Projects

One of the Sustainable Development Goals (SDG) of the UN on water is to increase access to clean water and sanitation facilities for communities where such facilities do not exist. The failure of water projects discussed here is the failure of projects on boreholes.

Importance of the water projects: A Nigerian, the author of this book, had the personal experience of travelling for about 3 miles to fetch water with a small clay pot in the nearest "clean" water source, in this case a spring; this was 6 miles to and fro. It was about 50 years ago when he lived as a boy of between 10 and 14 years of age in a village, Aro Mballa, Isuochi, in Okigwe district with his grandmother in the south-east of Nigeria. Since then, there has been a noticeable improvement in that there is now a pipe-borne potable water, which is centrally located in the marketplace, where water for household requirements could be fetched in buckets and pots. Similarly, in many other rural areas of sub-Saharan Africa, it remains the practice as of 2019 that people walked some 3–4 miles or more to the nearest borehole to get clean water for daily consumption in a small container, which could be about 4 litres. This could be the total water available to a family of about four or five for the day. This assumes that a borehole has been installed. In many areas, however, there are no such installations; the natives depend on water from streams, springs, rivers, etc.

It was certainly not surprising that international donor agencies had invested much money to help alleviate the problems since water is necessary for healthy living and survival. The International Institute for Environment and Development (IIED) reported that up to US$360 million had been spent on building boreholes and wells that then became useless because they were not maintained or fixed when they broke down. As a result, 50,000 water supply points were not functioning across rural Africa.

Causes of failures: Some causes of failure and abandonment of about 50,000 boreholes include the following:

- Poor construction and lack of skill and experience of maintaining the system.
- Poor supervision, failure caused by well users, and poor technology choice.

In a report by Casey and Carter of WaterAid Global [1], they stated: "People tend to make assumptions about why water sources fail and blame a lack of spare parts, financing, maintenance problems or climate change, for example. But often, the cause is not clear." Experience shows that the reported causes of failure are partial and not complete.

Suggested causes of the failures include:

- Operational malfunction
- Lack of support to ensure long-term sustainability
- Insufficient capacity building at the local level, such as skilled persons
- Failure to ensure availability of adequate resources, such as spares, fund, etc.
- Lack of project management training and support

Going forward: Mr. Hylton Ferreira, CEO at International Project Leadership Academy Namibia Ltd., made some statements in his report [2] which have been modified and interwoven with our comments as follows:

- As contained in the UN's 2030 SDG goals, there is a call for participation at the local level of the beneficiary communities with the visiting project teams in water and sanitation projects. It is relevant to observe that this call agrees with the strategy by Microsoft Corporation Limited on the successful "Digital Village" scheme in South Africa.
- He observes that funding initiatives from donors are commendable, but they often fall short as shown by real-life cases. The reason

is that establishing borehole and well infrastructure should not just stop with the physical implementation of the project because support after the implementation is necessary. There should be considerations for the provision of resources to ensure the continued operation of the scheme for many years after the project teams have left the site. These should include trained maintenance teams and readily available resources.

This is exactly the type of solution being espoused in this book, that is, planning from the start of the project to ensure that resources will be made available for the sustainability and operation of the project deliverables after the projects have been completed. This ensures that the benefits for which the deliverables have been produced are available over a period of 10 or more years, which is the planned lifetime of the project.

■ He suggests that national agencies in respective countries that receive funding for implementing water scheme should ensure that post-project resources are prepared for during the implementation. These include training and developing the skills of the operating teams and reliable and continual provision of funding and resources for operations within the planned lifetime of the water scheme. As already stated, this agrees with the practice in the successful "Digital Village" concept; that is, community members are co-opted as members of the project team from the start. They are trained and then work with the project and operation teams. They are therefore experienced in operating the system such that when the visiting project and operation team members complete their assignments and leave, the locals may have developed the confidence and competence to keep the deliverables operational.

He continued by suggesting that comprehensive project management training by proven training organisations can enhance the value of the investment. It is the observation of the author of this book that sadly many training courses to which local engineers and professionals are sent by the project implementing organisations are narrow and just tailored to enable them to perform their company tasks efficiently. Outside the confines of their jobs, the professionals know very little on the subject. For example, project engineers who are fresh from universities and other academic institutions should be taught the fundamentals of project management in the first instance before being trained on the implementation of a project on a gas compressor, electricity generator, etc.

In spite of the foregoing suggestion, this author remains thankful for the excellent training he received as a young engineer, in Nigeria and overseas, on power generation and supply and process engineering from firstly a visiting team of technical assistants from Ontario Hydro, Canada. This was followed by overseas training consisting of one-year long programme with the Electricity Supply Board of Ireland, Ireland. The two training programmes were such that even as he worked in other process industries such as oil and gas and steel production, he had the confidence to study and understand any process plants that he came across.

Money "Wasted" on Water Projects in Africa

This is a second report on water projects in Africa under the title: "Money 'Wasted' on Water Projects in Africa." It was written by Annie Kelly and appeared in Katine Chronicles blog [1].

Causes of failure:

1. The report criticises donors, governments and non-governmental organisations (NGOs) for installing boreholes and wells in rural Africa without providing resources and facilities for their long-term sustainability. It states that "hundreds of millions of dollars have been wasted on clean water projects in rural Africa."
2. The report continues, "[O]nly one third of water points built by NGOs in Senegal's Kaolack region are working and 58% of water points in northern Ghana are in disrepair." This was as in 2009.
3. The original author of the report, Mr. Jamie Skinner, writes that water points are often built by donors, governments and NGOs without fully consulting local people. As a result, they fail to find out "just how much it will cost to keep the boreholes clean and functioning over a sustained period of time."
4. He goes on to write that drilling a borehole in a rural community was analogous to asking people to run a cooperative private water supply. He continues:

   There is no point for an external agency coming in, putting in a drill-hole and then passing it over to the local community if they can't afford to maintain it over the next 10 or 20 years. There needs to be a proper assessment of just how much local people can finance these water points. It's not enough to just drill and walk away.

Comments: These problems have been encapsulated by the incident reported in Katine sub-county in north-east Uganda. In 2007, before the African Medical and Research Foundation (AMREF) and Farm-Africa began their development work in Katine, worms were found in the polluted water supply at the village of Abia, next to the Emuru swamp. This was from a badly constructed and poorly maintained shallow well, dug by a charity; it was full of soil and animal faeces and was making local people sick. This was the sorry state of wells which had been produced and passed on to the locals without any adequate and effective arrangement for their maintenance and sustenance.

New Operations Strategy

AMREF developed the following strategy for their new operations:

■ Training of local communities to operate and maintain the new safe water points that have been established in the sub-county since the project began.
■ Water and sanitation committees have been set up to monitor the new boreholes that have been dug and to contact newly trained hand-pump mechanics if one breaks down.
■ The committees meet regularly with village health teams to discuss needs.
■ It is planned that everyone who uses the boreholes and wells will contribute financially to their long-term upkeep.

Submission by Mr. Bob Reed, Water Engineer, and the then Senior Programme Manager, Water Education and Development Centre (WEDC), Loughborough University, Loughborough, UK.

Mr. Reed was a water engineer with over 30 years' experience and had worked on dozens of water projects in Africa and Asia. As AMREF worked on boreholes in Katine, he talked to Anne Perkins about the best way to help small rural communities get access to safe water as well as the problems of sustainability. The title of his submission was: "Water debate: are boreholes sustainable?"

He made the following submission which was reported on Monday, 25 February 2008:

- "Rural water," Reed believes, "cannot be sustained without external support – any more than urban water supplies can."
- Without this, the boreholes were simply unsustainable.

Causes of failure and expected problems: Both Reed and AMREF were well experienced on the problem of boreholes that fell into disuse because of the following reasons:

- Spare parts were not available.
- Lack of trained mechanics because those trained had left for better work in town.
- The water management committee had fallen out.

To solve these problems, AMREF started training mechanics and setting up committees, encouraging a sense of ownership.

Funding problem: However, Reed, the water engineer, no longer believed that boreholes were the best option for providing water in a poor rural community. Like AMREF, he argued for the widest possible range of sources – harvesting of rainwater as well instead of only boreholes and hand pumps. But the schemes often failed because of wider influences in the locality; these could be political. An example of local political conditions that adversely affected the water supply system was the incident in Uganda that impacted on the revenue of the local district administration who used to subsidise local agents who supplied spare parts for hand pumps. But in the last elections before February 2008, the president of Uganda reportedly promised to abolish the poll tax which was the district administration's only source of income. With this done, there has been reportedly no subsidy for buying parts.

Maintenance problem: Rural water problems are aggravated by low population densities which mean relatively few boreholes. AMREF is installing eight in Katine. That is not enough, Reed argues, to support a mechanic. Nor is there evidence that there are enough boreholes in the wider region to provide a living for a mechanic. And even if there were, the chances are that the pumps could be of different makes. Efforts to standardise them have failed.

Success of Boreholes in Ghana Government Support Scheme

Reed could talk of some successful borehole projects in Ghana. They succeeded because they relied on the government, which provided support, training and maintenance to keep boreholes running effectively. This report is supported by Rossiter, Owusu, et al. [3]. They report that "[t]o reduce child mortality and improve healthcare in Ghana, boreholes and wells are being installed across the country by the private sector, NGO's and the Ghanaian government." They report that most installation costs are generally paid by the government or NGOs, while the maintenance is expected to be covered by the community. At least 58% of the communities had a water payment system in place, either an annual fee or one-off fee or "pay-as-you-fetch." The annual fee was between £0.3 and £2.1, while the boreholes had a water collection fee of £0.07–0.7/m^3; many wells were free.

Comments

It is clear from the foregoing reports that water supply through boreholes could be successful in Africa if supported with appropriate funding, supervisory committee and maintenance resources.

Questions

- Please list from this chapter the guidelines that you can elicit for successful long-term operation of boreholes.
- Also, list causes of failures of the rural water supply schemes built in Africa.

References

1. Casey and Carter, WaterAid Global Annie Kelly, "Money 'wasted' on water projects in Africa," 26 March 2009, *The Guardian*, https://www.theguardian.com/society/katineblog/2009/mar/26/water-projects-wasted-money

2. Hylton Ferreira, "Failure of projects on Boreholes and wells (developing community water sources), at Jul 2016 Cost : $360M," CEO at International Project Leadership Academy Namibia Ltd. International Donor Agencies – Africa, 15 November 2016.

3. M. A. Rossiter Helfrid, Peter A. Owusu, et al. "Chemical drinking water quality in Ghana: water costs and scope for advanced treatment," *Science of The Total Environment*, Vol. 408, No. 11, 1 May 2010, Pages 2378–2386.

Chapter 7

Failures in the Electricity Industry

From research and operational experience, causes of failures include the following:

1. **Low generating capacity:** There are few active electricity generating stations or plants. Some of the older ones are obsolete and cannot be supported. As a result, the generating capacity is low. It is so low that it is a major drawback to economic development. For example, in 2015, Spain, with a population of about 46 million, had an installed generation capacity of about 101,000 MW, while some major countries of sub-Saharan Africa, with a population of over 600 million, had a total capacity of about 70,000 MW. Nigeria had 25 power plants and a total installed capacity of 12,341 MW, with the highest recorded peak at 5,090 MW on 26 April 2018. South Africa had a generating capacity of 51,300 MW with a population of 58 million. It was estimated that 130,000 MW was the minimum installed capacity that should be aimed at for Nigeria to have a comparable capacity like South Africa. This is certainly below the standard of the developed nations for a country with a population of about 200 million. Yet this cannot be achieved immediately but over some years [1].

2. **Low investment in electricity:** According to the Nigeria Power Minister in 2018, Babatunde Fashola, although the country had expended fund that might appear sizeable, the money so far spent is inadequate to address the current challenges. The Minister said:

When I hear that we have spent a lot of money on the power sector, I say that we haven't spent enough money and that is why we are still talking about the need for investments to come in. Yes, what we have spent may look sizeable but it doesn't provide enough power for our consumption as a nation. People say: "Oh, we spend money but there is nothing to show for it." There is something to show for it. The plants are there. The total installed capacity that the nation can look forward to today is 12,000MW. That is what we bought with our money – that is the installed capacity.

Note that an exception has been made in writing the minister's name instead of omitting it because he is correct and constructive in these statements [2].

Poor planning: He continued:

However, the plants are not producing 12,000MW of power because either pipelines are broken, or gas supply was not properly planned or because evacuation was not properly planned, or other reasons. Those are the challenges that we have responsibility now to deal with.

3. **Ageing transmission and distribution equipment:** As already stated, some of the transmission and distribution lines are old and needed being replaced. Nigeria, in 2016, could only transmit 5000 MW. In May 2018, the Minister, Fashola stated that the transmission capacity was increased to 7000 MW.

In 2018 and 2019, the transformers, both grid and distribution transformers, are old and are serving longer than their designed duration of service. To worsen the situation, the transformers, especially distribution transformers, are overloaded due to illegal connections, which make them carry more current than they are designed for. Sometimes, these explode and cut off power supply to all the consumers they serve.

The costs of building new electricity generators, grid lines, substations and transformers are quite high. These are some of the reasons why Africa is in darkness. There is therefore a business justification for resort to solar and renewable energy. It is also the case that fossil fuels such as oil, coal and natural gas used for electricity generation cause much pollution due to the emission of carbon dioxide. This explains why many developed nations resort to renewable energy sources which create little or no pollution.

Failure to maintain plants for years: Two examples are given below of plants which were not maintained for many years and their adverse effects on the national power supply.

1. A hydro power plant in Nigeria was commissioned in 1985 with six generators to provide 540 MW of power. The turbines were to be over-hauled as scheduled maintenance once every five to six years. This was never done for 31 years, until it was handed over in 2013, in the after-math of the privatisation. The first overhaul was done in May 2016 [2].
2. A gas-fired power plant in Nigeria was commissioned in 1985. It had six units with total capacity of 1,320 MW (i.e. 6×220 MW). When it was pri-vatised in 2013, it had only two functional units, that is about 400 MW generating capacity. In December 2015, the six units were reactivated and restored to operation [2].

Wrong location of power plant – poor project planning: There is a 215 MW gas-fired power plant in Nigeria, which is located several hundred kilo-metres away from gas sources. As of 2019, it has not been in operation for many years because of no gas supply. The pipelines had been vandalised. Efforts were on for alternative and sustainable fuel supply. The government has learnt not to site power plants far away from their fuel source [2].

Poor Power Supply Causes Poor Economic Growth

In the paper, Powering Africa Report [3], the authors stated that there is a direct correlation between economic growth and electricity supply. Sub-Saharan Africa is in short supply of electricity. Even in 2019 and in the foreseeable future, the region's power sector is significantly underdevel-oped at energy access, installed capacity or overall consumption. Providing economic and social requirements of the region depends on the ability of the government and investors to develop the continent's huge electricity capacity.

It is reported that the region is worst in the world from an electricity-access point of view. It has 13% of the world's population, but 48% of the share of the global population is without access to electricity. Another region with poor electricity access, but better than sub-Saharan, is South Asia. It has 23% of the world's population, and 34% of the people are without access to electricity.

In effect, almost 600 million people in sub-Saharan Africa lack access to electricity. Only seven countries – Cameroon, Côte d'Ivoire, Gabon, Ghana, Namibia, Senegal and South Africa – have electricity access rates exceeding 50%. The rest of the region has an average grid access rate of just 20%. Moreover, even when there is access to electricity, there is certainly not enough to go round.

It is reported that in sub-Saharan Africa, the electric utility infrastructure necessary for large-scale energy power plants is lacking. For example, in Kenya, at least 50 power outages occur each year. It is apt to comment, with all due respect, that within the past 20 or more years to 2019, such number of outages could occur in a month in some countries in sub-Saharan Africa, such as Nigeria. Across Africa, 500 million people lack access to electricity. "African countries will need to spend at least six percent of their GDP on energy over the next 10 years to keep up with their economic growth. It is therefore clear that a number of technologies (both traditional and new) will need to be applied," says Dana Rysankova, a World Bank senior energy specialist for Africa, in the report's press release [4].

It is estimated that about 70% of the people live in the rural areas. Electricity access is limited and substantially confined to the urban areas; even then, power utilities are struggling to expand access and improve reliability of their supply. The electrification rates of public institutions like schools and health centres, and water pumping and irrigation facilities are also low. This statistic shows the enormity of the problem and underscores the need for alternative power supply sources.

Renewable energy resources are widely available and should be exploited. Off-grid solar energy products offer a better solution for reasons which include the following:

■ With advancement in solar technologies, stand-alone off-grid solar now has the potential to provide electricity access in sub-Saharan Africa, especially for, consumers who are far from the grid network. The capital cost of the power generating stations and the erection or extension of grid network is such that one cannot predict the number of years when grid supply will be connected to them.
■ Even those who are expected to get access to grid network in a couple of years' time can use stand-alone solar systems and not burn kerosene,

wood, standby diesel generators and candles, or live in darkness as they wait for their grid connection.

■ Dependence and use of these pollutants contribute to over 600,000 deaths annually from household air pollution.

■ Millions of Africans, including those in oil-rich Nigeria, live in economies where per capita electricity supply is enough to light a single 100 W light bulb continuously for 60 days a year. This is said to be equivalent to the average power consumed per person in Africa every year; it is said to be only enough to power one 100 W light bulb for only three hours a day! This is according to a World Bank report, "The World Bank: Fact Sheet: Infrastructure in Sub-Saharan Africa, 2013." It is therefore necessary to invest in affordable renewable energy sources.

Questions

■ How reliable is the electricity supply to sub-Saharan Africa?
■ How do you justify your answer?
■ What are the reasons for the current situation?
■ Are renewable energy sources needed? Please give your reasons.

References

1. O. Chima Okereke, "Roadmap for sustainable power supply in Nigeria," *PM World Journal*, Vol. VIII, No. IX, October 2019, www.pmworldjournal.com
2. Babatunde Fashola, "Nigeria's power generation will increase by 2,000MW in 2016," *Premium Times*, 3 February 2016.
3. Antonio Castellano, Adam Kendall, Mikhail Nikomarov and Tarryn Swemmer, "Powering Africa," *Report* – February 2015.
4. Ben Black, Worldwatch Institute – vision for sustainable growth, "African renewable energy gains attention," 12 September 2008.

Chapter 8

Renewable Energy Projects: Failure and Successes

In this chapter, discussions on some projects in renewable energy are presented. Causes of the initial failure of the projects and subsequent successes are reviewed. The chapter is started with this quotation: "Unacceptable and Irresponsible Failures in the number of African Renewable Energy Projects." The Director* of the African Renewable Energy Forum held in Senegal in 2008 was said to have made this comment. Actually, his very words were: "The number of failed renewable energy projects in Africa over the last 20 years is unacceptable and verging on the irresponsible. These failed projects have set back development by raising aspirations and then failing to deliver" [1].

Africa is rich in renewable natural resources: Africa has a great potential to become a gold mine in clean energy through its abundance of renewable energy in solar and wind resources. However, there are obstacles to overcome. These include wars, political instability, poor infrastructure and financial resources. Further, the World Bank reported that the renewable energy potential for Africa could provide more than 170 GW of additional power generation capacity; this was more than double the power generation capacity in the continent in 2018–2019. Such renewable energy projects could prevent the production of some 740 million tons of carbon dioxide annually. The total cost of such projects was estimated at $157 billion. The projects were said to be economically viable if carbon revenues were added, explained Massaba Thioye, World Bank senior energy specialist, at the meeting in Dakar, Senegal, from 3 to 5 September 2008. In attendance were

---

* Name of the person has been deliberately omitted.

officers of the UN and World Bank as well as business leaders who discussed strategies for "Clean Development Mechanism" (CDM) projects on the continent. These were said to be greenhouse gas reducing initiatives that industrialised countries could support as compensation for their excessive emissions. A theme at the conference was the possibility of engaging in future CDM projects under a successor agreement to the Kyoto Protocol.

Problem of Low Investments in Africa

It was reported that Africa had received the least investment from the $7 billion annual CDM market. Only 0.02% or 27 out of 1,156 CDM projects were registered in Africa since 2002 when the European Union began trading "carbon credits" through its Emissions Trading Scheme. Yvo de Boer, Executive Secretary of the UN Framework Convention on Climate Change (UNFCCC), presented this information to the carbon forum. Further, sub-Saharan Africa could receive only 1.4% of the 3,700 CDM projects worldwide as of 1 September 2008.

Again, during the Africa Energy Forum in June 2008, participants focused almost entirely on fossil fuel-based energy sources, according to the World Council for Renewable Energy Chairman.* It was he who complained that the forum lacked a renewable energy focus. This prompted the Conference Director† to respond that "Africa's future energy growth is reliant on conventional power sources and that the renewable energy hype has only provided set-backs." He followed up this statement with an email in which he wrote:

> To claim that Africa's problems of poverty would be alleviated by relying on renewable energy is folly, the number of failed renewable energy projects in Africa over the last 20 years is unacceptable and verging on the irresponsible. These failed projects have set back development by raising aspirations and then failing to deliver.

Lack of Access to, and Grossly Inadequate Reliable Grid Supply in Nigeria [2, 3]

Some 100 million of Nigeria's estimated 154 million people did not have access to nationally provided electricity according to a 2005 report by the

---

* Names deliberately omitted.
† Names deliberately omitted.

Energy Sector Management Assistance Program (ESMAP), a global technical assistance partnership administered by the World Bank. The federal government privatised electricity in 2005, and though the newly reorganised Power Holding Company of Nigeria (PHCN) slowly increased capacity each year, some economically depressed areas still did not have enough residents who could afford to pay for the service.

As published on 10 November 2015, in the *Vanguard News*, a Nigerian newspaper and online version of the Vanguard, 75% Nigerians lacked access to regular power. Despite the huge investments made in the energy sector since the privatisation of the Power Holding Company of Nigeria, PHCN, about 75% of the Nigerian population reportedly still lived without access to regular electricity supply. According to the Nigerian Association of Energy Economists, NAEE, despite statistics indicating that 45% of the country's population was then connected to the national grid, regular supply was said to be restricted to just about 25% of the population. The NAEE therefore raised concern on economic redundancy in these parts of the country because of the importance of energy to economic development. The National President* of The NAEE made this point at the 2015 World Energy Day, 10 November.

The motivation to introduce renewable energy resources was to provide environmentally friendly power supply to businesses and homes given the inability of the national power supply to meet their needs. Businesses, large and small, were being adversely affected. The researchers who wrote the report on Nigeria and renewable energy claimed that the average Nigerian household might have access to less than 655 KW hours a year of electricity, compared with a global average of nearly 3,300 KW hours a year, according to the World Energy Council Energy Efficiency Indicator in 2014.

Grossly Deficient and Lack of Electricity Supply Extends the Cycle of Poverty

"Nigeria's aspiration for industrialization cannot be achieved or poverty reduced significantly without a reliable source of cheap energy," said Dr. Patrick M. Kormawa, Regional Director for the United Nations Industrial Development Organization, (UNIDO), in the Nigeria's office. Speaking at a meeting in June 2011, he said, "Countries without reliable power supply per

---

* Name omitted deliberately.

capita happen to be the poorest countries in the world. Clearly, there is a correlation between poverty and energy access."

"Rural areas which are remote from the grid and/or have low consumption or low power purchase potential will not be attractive to private power investors," said Abubakar S. Sambo, Director-General of the Energy Commission of Nigeria. "Such areas may remain unserved for the distant future."

Generally, it is estimated that the nation has as much as 90 percent deficiency in electricity supply. In off-grid areas where some 50 percent of Nigerians live, access to electricity is practically zero. In on-grid areas, power outages are still a recurrent theme, and this has continued to pose serious constraints to economic development.

Nigeria's Solar Projects: A Mixture of Failures and Successes

An Example of a Failed Renewable Energy Project in Nigeria [4]

Five years after its installation, a Lagos State Government-sponsored solar project at the Osinowo village of Bishop Kodji in 2006 was not in operation. This was the first of its kind in the state built to provide electric power for water pumps, fish driers, streetlamps, etc. It was to give the small fishing and boat-carving community's 5,000 residents access to potable drinking water, to secure their sandy streets and to strengthen their fishing economy. The photovoltaic system did not work as envisaged.

To help understand its geography, the island is just 15 minutes by boat from Lagos Island, one of wealthiest and most developed areas in the country. According to the reporter, "We don't know what's going on," said Azime Anthony, a traditional leader in Bishop Kodji. "It only worked for about three months, and then it stopped. All the places where we are supposed to have light are dark and they never came back to try to fix any of it."

To reactive the failed system at Bishop Kodji, in 2006, the Lagos State Government operatives stepped in and installed 300 W photovoltaic (PV) panels at two sites. The system was to supply power to the community building, the primary school, a church, a mosque and a water pump that was installed at the village well to lift water into an overhead tank. This was according to a report on the project by Adenike Boyo, Director of Science and Technology at the Directorate of Policy, Programmes and Promotion for the state of Lagos. The project was praised after this repair as a cost-effective triumph. "These people are living off grid," said Tunji Olagunju, the engineer in charge of the Bishop Kodji project. He continued:

> There was no possibility of getting the national power supply from Power Holding company of Nigeria (PHCN) to them even in the next 50 to 60 years, but they too must benefit from government; and that is why Lagos state decided that they had to give them alternative energy which, in this case, is solar.

In view of its relatively small budget, the project appeared to be the perfect solution to the state's rural electrification issues. "It costs about 150 million naira (then about $1.2 million) to connect each village to the national grid, while the solar energy project costs only about 10 million naira (about $83,000) per village," Kadri Hamzat, State Commissioner of Science and Technology, explained in an interview with journalists at the project's launch.

After the initial success at Bishop Kodji, Lagos State officials introduced similar projects in nine other communities. But problems soon emerged, the first, apparently resulting from local jealousies. Residents say that once news of their solar installation spread, people from neighbouring communities came and sabotaged the solar units. State workers replaced cut wires, only to be called out again when the panels failed a second time due to an undetermined mechanical failure. According to reports, residents complained that state workers had not returned for routine servicing since then.

Cause of Failure: Poor and Inadequate Maintenance

"It wasn't something that we could predict," Olagunju said. "We have gone out several times to fix the issues that we find. But most of the problems come from poor maintenance by the residents," he said. Residents, some of whom were trained to maintain the equipment, say state officials are to blame. Dansu, one of the trained residents, wrote:

> We went to Alausa (the government centre), we wrote letters that they needed to come. This thing is not working, because when it was working, we were all enjoying it and we were happy. We wrote and kept persisting; they didn't answer us. We called over the phone and we even went there in person; they never answered us.

The residents of Bishop Kodji still hope that the solar installations that promised to change their lives will work again. "We are fishermen," Anthony said. He continued:

> We catch fish, we treat them, and then we sell them to our own people. We see that the government is trying to do something for us. But we need them to do more. We need a hospital. We need a better school. And we need light.

Five years later, the panels still did not work. Efforts to ascertain its situation at this time of writing in 2018 proved abortive.

Other failures: It was reported then that some solar streetlights in Lagos and Abuja had broken down. The experience of Lagos was echoed in more than a dozen Nigerian states, including Sokoto, Bornu, Nasarawa, Bayelsa and Delta. The failure in Sokoto prompted the state government to abandon its other solar projects, along with the accompanying federal funding, and instead tried to connect the state to the national grid. But that was a $22 million project that should take decades to complete, according to Alhaji Garb Umar Kyadawa, the then Special Adviser to the Sokoto State Governor on rural electrification.

These experiences appeared to eliminate all hope for Nigeria to extend electricity access through renewable energy. However, there were significant successes elsewhere in the nation, including in a community about 700 miles (1,160 kilometres) from Bishop Kodji, in Jigawa, a state on the northern border of Nigeria. The successes will be discussed, but reasons for the failure will be explored next.

Causes of Failure of Renewable Energy Projects in Nigeria

They include the following:

1. Poor planning due to lack of project planning skills by planners. For example, it is said that the planners lacked information such as:
   - The number of users to be supplied with the power generated
   - Suitable location for the planned solar parks for the target customers
   - How the power from the project should be connected to the grid
   - Absence of adequate government support

- Poor arrangement made for training, maintenance and management of the delivered renewable energy supply

2. As of 2018, there was also the necessity for better government control of the renewable energy market. To expatiate, the Editor* of Nigeria Alternative Energy reported that there was an influx of fake solar panels from China to Ghana. According to him, this could have been prevented if there had been an effective government control. He continues: "Governments in Africa are still finding it difficult to officially adopt the technology, and this has greatly affected its uptake."

Successful Renewable Energy Project in Nigeria [4]

It is considered necessary to discuss some successes attained, if nothing to show that it was not just a case of failure all through. It is also relevant to understand why the successes were achieved.

There are successful solar projects in northern Nigeria, particularly in Jigawa State, and other parts of the country. They provide not only water but also a microenterprise centre. They provide power supply to healthcare and educational services. Research supports our finding in other industries such as water. One of which is that a difference between success and failure is it is not enough to install equipment; the power systems need to be planned carefully, the implemented system has to be funded adequately and sustained for the long-term. The detailed account of a success story in which these suggestions have been applied is given next.

A Bright Spot in Jigawa

In 2001, Ibrahim Turaki, who was then Governor of Jigawa state, obtained funding assistance from the Japanese government to launch a full-scale rural electrification project, with additional funding assistance from the United States Agency for International Development (USAID) and the United States Department of Energy. The sponsors invested $450,000, more than five times the amount spent at Bishop Kodji. The Jigawa project was implemented and maintained by the Solar Electric Light Fund (SELF), a non-governmental organisation based in Washington, D.C., that has been spearheading solar

---

* Name deliberately omitted.

projects in the developing world for 21 years. The SELF-directed scheme launched with bigger goals and more risks than Bishop Kodji and has yielded greater successful results.

"We wanted to create a comprehensive project that would touch every aspect of their lives," said Robert Freling, Executive Director of SELF.

> We provided power for a water-pumping system that pushed clean water into the village. Women can turn on a tap and have fresh water in the town centre without walking miles to fetch it. There is a microenterprise centre, street lighting, lights for 20 homes, a portable pump that they can take from field to field and water their crops. It's really remarkable.

The system in Jigawa powers vaccine refrigerators and lights health centres, schools and religious centres. At night, because of the electricity, villagers can receive emergency care in the health centre, primary schools double as adult education centres and villagers gather in the cool evenings under solar-powered streetlights.

The SELF website reports that because of the steady access to power in Jigawa, residents were able to open a computer technology trade school and became the first state in northern Nigeria to create a satellite-based broadband Internet and communications system to link all local government districts.

"(After Jigawa), we got requests from pretty much every state in Nigeria looking to implement something similar," Freling said. He believed that the difference between what happened at Bishop Kodji and what happened in Jigawa was in both the planning and the maintenance.

"Sustainability is our primary concern," Freling said. "If you have a project that's well thought out, funded and executed, you have a project that should last not months but years. There should always be a sustainability plan in mind from the beginning."

Going Forward

The Energy Sector Management Assistance Program (ESMAP) predicted that the number of Nigerians without access to electricity should increase over time. It suggested that local photovoltaic systems have the potential to fill in the energy shortfall, while the federal government shores up national energy production and policy. It observed that the role of solar energy in meeting

Africa's energy needs had been undermined by misinformation, lack of technology, bad experiences and the negative perceptions that had risen in situations such as the Bishop Kodji project.

"If the government has a bad experience or hears about a failure, it affects the attitude of officials," Freling said. "It's easy for projects to be poorly executed or poorly maintained and that taints their perception" [4].

Comments and "Turning of the Tide" in the Renewable Energy Industry

Following the reports so far on the many failures of the renewable energy projects in Nigeria, it should be admitted that there was some truth in the already reported dismissive comments by an energy Conference Director* in 2008. The comment was that "the number of failed renewable energy projects in Africa over the last 20 years is unacceptable and verging on the irresponsible." He was quite correct in as much as the absence of an arrangement to support and maintain the installed renewable energy power supplies that led to their failure and abandonment. They constituted irresponsible investments and sources of loss of public fund.

However, the tide has turned for good. With the kind intervention of the UK Department for International Development (UK DFIF) in the solar power industry in Nigeria, there is a new chapter of success stories which will be presented from the next paragraph.

Why Should There Be a Section on Successes in a Book That Discusses Failed Projects?

It is simply the fact that the topic "lessons learned" is an important aspect of project management. When lessons learned from the mistakes and failures of a failed project are applied in the implementation of a new project such that it is successful, then it is noteworthy. Its success underlines and justifies the fact that the successful approach should be used for such implementations going forward.

In other words, the successes attained in the implementation of solar projects in Nigeria and other African and developing countries demonstrate

---

* Name withheld deliberately.

that the methods used so successfully should be used in future solar projects. They show what should be avoided and what should be copied.

Successful Developments in the Solar Power

While it has not been possible to ascertain the situation now of the solar power supply in Bishop Kodji, there have been many successful renewable energy projects in Lagos and other states of Nigeria. Some of them are described in the following paragraphs. The interest should be in the arrangement with the UK DFID and other international organisations that have led to success in the project deliverables.

Successful Streetlights in Lagos, 2016

The Editor of the *Guardian* newspaper reported on 18 March 2016, that TECNO, maker of mobile telecoms gadgets in Nigeria, had installed 88 solar-powered streetlights around the computer village and environs in the Ikeja local government area of Lagos State. The "Light up Ikeja" project was concluded on 21 January 2016. The Chairman of Ogunbiyi Community Development Association, Ikeja local government area, Adeniyi Olasoji, said the project could not have come at a better time when the economic situation in the country was biting hard and state governments were trying to cut down costs. It had provided constant power supply and improved security around the electronics market at night.

Comments: While in 2018, it may be too early to comment on the sustainability of the project deliverables – in this case, the streetlights – the arrangement between the Lagos State Government and the UK DFID so far has ensured their maintenance. More successful project deliverables are discussed in the subsequent paragraphs.

Lagos State and UK Department for International Development (UK DFID)

Lagos State Government jointly commissioned and funded its Renewable Energy Initiative with the UK DFID. It was planned to deliver 5 MW solar energy to education and health facilities in the state by the end of 2015. It should deliver 213 solar power systems, ranging in size from 9 KW to 185 KW, to 183 rural, riverine locations including boarding schools and health centres. At the time of the project inception, all rural schools and hospitals depend on diesel- and petrol-powered generators. According to the Project Manager,* the project was to be completed in October 2015.

A report on progress in Lagos solar power is presented in a few sections from here.

Building the Market for Solar Power in Nigeria

The report in 2018 is that Nigeria has huge potential for solar electricity. With the trend showing the reduction of the cost of solar power and that Nigeria's need for affordable, reliable and clean electric power has remained high, Solar Nigeria Programme is currently working on solar projects in Nigeria. It was launched in 2014 and was being funded by the UK Department for International Development (DFID) and was collaborating with other donors and Nigeria's federal and state governments. The programme works with solar companies, local banks and international finance to help businesses, institutions and households get access to solar power on terms they can afford. It also works in partnership with state governments to bring solar power to key health and education facilities in areas of the country where the need is greatest. It works directly with companies that manufacture, install and finance solar energy systems.

The Programme Approach

It tries to grow the solar energy market in Nigeria by using the following approach, as quoted from their publication:

> Supplying technical assistance to companies;
>> Providing facilities for affordable consumer credit; and
>> Delivering demonstration projects that show that well-designed solar systems are sustainable, save money, and reduce greenhouse gasses.

---

* Name withheld.

Providing grants and technical assistance to well-qualified companies that are already in the Nigerian solar market, or that seek to enter it.

Lagos Solar Project: The following achievements have been reported:

Reported much improvement in schools and health clinics: Lagos Solar in 2016–2017 was then Nigeria's largest distributed social solar programme, providing nearly 5 MW of solar power in total. It supplied electricity to 175 secondary schools and 11 primary healthcare centres (PHCs) in rural, riverine and peri-urban areas of Lagos State. Each school or clinic was equipped with one or several systems of 5–25 KW capacity. The systems were configured to meet each facility's power needs.

Lagos Solar was a joint venture between Lagos State Electricity Board (LSEB) and Solar Nigeria. Lagos State Government and DFID contributed GBP15 million each towards the project. LSEB owns and maintains the completed installations.

Lagos Solar installations were commissioned in three phases between December 2014 and April 2016. They already had a major impact on recipient schools and clinics. Schools reported improved student participation, teacher and staff morale and ability to add and use equipment ranging from classroom fans to computer lab facilities. Clinics reported improved conditions for staff and patients and were registering an increase in patient numbers, including more mothers coming to give birth in safe and clean surroundings – particularly for night-time deliveries. In schools and clinics, the solar installation allowed a drastic reduction in the use of diesel or petrol generators, resulting in less air and noise pollution, and the reallocation of scarce fund for other uses directly related to teaching or patient care.

At Lagos clinics, solar turned health care around: The impact of the new system can be appreciated in the following anecdote.

When Mrs. Suliyat Iyabo came to Ita-Elewa Primary Healthcare Centre (PHC) to give birth to her second child, she thought she knew the routine. After all, her first child, three-year-old Ruth, had been born at this same clinic. So she expected that she had to pay for candles or for petrol to run the clinic's generator.

Instead to her surprise, the lights were on – and they stayed on through her delivery at 3 a.m. Still, Suliyat was sceptical. "After giving birth, I was expecting the nurse to tell me to bring petrol to replace what was used for me," she said. But the nurses made no such request. Finally, she could not contain her curiosity. "I asked the nurse how come they still have light in their area." She replied, 'My dear, na solar be this.'" This means, "My dear, the electricity is from solar power."

Until recently, clinics like Ita-Elewa had no choice but to ask patients to contribute to keep the lights and machinery running. That was why Suliyat had to bring petrol for the generator the first time she gave birth. Since 2016, however, Ita-Elewa has a 186kWp solar photovoltaic (PV) installation that ensures the clinic's main functions get reliable power supply around the clock. The PV system is part of Lagos Solar, an initiative of the Lagos State Government and the UK Department for International Development, which has equipped 11 clinics and 172 public secondary schools in rural and peri-urban parts of Lagos State.

Positive impact: The impact of solar has been unmistakable, not just for patients like Mrs. Iyabo but also for the clinic's staff of doctors, nurses and medical and laboratory technicians. At Ita-Elewa, the Nursing Matron, Mrs. Maupe Johnson, is still new to the clinic, having been transferred there when the previous matron retired. Her previous clinic did not have the benefit of solar installations. Mrs. Johnson said the difference in working conditions was striking. In the past, she had to make emergency deliveries at night and in the dark because of the unreliable power situation. Not so at Ita-Elewa. "We don't use the generator anymore," she said. "The light has not 'offed.' It is 24 hours." This means that the light has not gone off and is on for 24 hours daily.

Reliable power changed everything for a clinic like Ita-Elewa, which was the first point of basic medical services for a large population in a 5 kilometre radius in the Ikorodu area of Lagos State. The clinic was busier, as news of the improved conditions quickly spread around. Patient numbers rose up across clinics where Lagos Solar had set up systems, as people chose them over other facilities. "With solar, people are coming here instead of other clinics," said Mrs. Johnson. "The workload is too much o!"

But with added work came improved morale, and even colleagues came from other sites. For example, "At times, other nurses come even when they are off duty to use the light, and we put them to work," said Mrs. Johnson. Safety had improved as well. As in many parts of the state, Ita-Elewa used to have problems with "area boys" (hooligans) who would hassle patients and staff on their way to or from the facility. For nurses, coming to work at night could be dangerous. But now, said Mrs. Johnson, "It's much safer to come to work at the clinic at night, with the lights on."

Similar improvements were taking place at the entire 11 Primary Healthcare Centre (PHCs) that were now equipped with Lagos Solar installations. At Eredo PHC in Epe town, in eastern Lagos State, the pharmacist reported that even the local general hospital had begun stocking some of its medicines in the PHC's always-running refrigerators.

The patient experience had improved dramatically as well. "I no dey fear to go PHC again as I know say fan go blow me for there as I dey wait doctor," said one patient. "Even doctor sef, fan go blow am so she no go dey vex when e dey ask question." Translating the statements by the patients into normal English language – the patient says that she has no anxiety going to wait for doctor at the clinic because she knows that with the electricity supply on, electric fan will be blowing fresh air on her and on the doctor. This will make the doctor ask questions to patients without being annoyed.

"Since solar has been providing us with constant power, we have been able to store test samples and get more accurate results," added a Lab Technician at Eredo PHC. "Most importantly, we are happy to see that patients can get all their tests while waiting, without going to external laboratories. This improves morale and we can provide good service."

Acknowledgement: Lagos Solar, Success Stories

Progress and Improvement in Education as Solar Power Provides Affordable Energy for Classrooms, IT Lessons and Much More

David Nwandiogo, 13 years of age, developed his love for computers after an Easter visit to an uncle's house where he had unrestricted access to a desktop machine. He quickly understood how to use it and how to get useful information from Google. When David returned to Government Model Junior Secondary School in Owutu, in the Ikorodu area of Lagos State, he was keen to join the ICT (information and communications technology) class to build on his interest. But there was a problem: no electricity. With no power arriving from the grid, the school could only afford fuel to turn on its generator for one or two hours a day. This made it next to impossible to hold ICT classes. Lessons were rushed and combined, and everyone, students and teachers alike, was frustrated.

"There is little you can achieve in darkness," said the Vice Principal, Mr. Adejobi Aderemi. But fortunately for David and his friends, the electricity situation at the school has improved completely since the Lagos Solar project set up a 25 KW solar photovoltaic (PV) system on site, right on the school's grounds. Now, the classrooms, administrative offices and hostels have power for their crucial needs, making resort to the generator almost unnecessary.

In the ICT room, all 20 computers can be on now whenever needed. "The ICT room is available, the computers have Internet and the students can access the web," said Mr. Aderemi. "They can do their assignments at any time."

Lagos Solar, in this case, was a joint project of Solar Nigeria and the Lagos State Electricity Board (LSEB), installed systems in some 32 public secondary schools in early 2015, followed by another 140 schools in 2016. More than a year after installation began, rigorous monitoring provided evidence of glowing results.

Remarkable progress: Schools reported increases in enrolment, and most importantly, recorded marked improvements in performance on the Senior Secondary Certificate Examination (SSCE). Staff morale and enthusiasm to work became higher as well.

In addition, 63% of schools with computer labs reported improvements in the operations of the labs, while 68% of schools with integrated science labs also experienced better use of labs after the solar installations.

Maintenance Arrangement of Deliverables

While the on-site installations belonged to LSEB, the school in Owutu had its own energy officer, Mr. Kasali Olamide, whom the power board trained on how to monitor the systems and ensure their appropriate use. The systems were turned off at midnight to charge the batteries and avoid overwork. After an energy audit, all the light bulbs in the school were retrofitted to energy-saving LED bulbs. At monthly maintenance sessions, Mr. Olamide reminded the staff of how to take care of the system and not to plug in heavy energy-draining devices such as heaters or air conditioners.

Complying with these cautions was easy enough affirmed the students and staff. After all, continuous power from solar was a world away from the conditions they experienced before. "Before solar, if there was no light we couldn't read," said Fathia Abdulkareem, a junior secondary school third-year student. "We would try to read during afternoon prep or we would use torchlights, but since we have solar, we can read during night prep." [Prep is a private study class by students outside the official school hours.]

The school's house mistress, Mrs. Rose Sharon, agreed. "Solar doesn't make noise, and the students are encouraged to read," she said. "We see lots of improvements in their general well-being and education."

Observations and Comments

From this report on Solar Nigeria in some parts of Lagos State, it is sad that 24 hours' availability of power supply which is the norm in developed countries is a novelty in our schools and clinics in the years 2018, 2019, when this book is being written, and earlier. It reveals a lot about the sufferings that most of the people in Africa have to live with. It is a deliberate decision to include these anecdotes which contain real-life conversations by our people because they are discussing their experiences which show the impact, indeed the differences, that solar power is making in their lives. It underscores the need for more investments in the solar industry. It also shows that when investments are properly made with the support and maintenance facilities, and resources provided, native Africans can maintain the installed systems and enjoy their benefits.

Acknowledgement: Information in the preceeding paragraphs was taken from Solar Power Nigeria, contact information: info@solar-ng.com, www.solar-ng.com.

Renewable Energy in Other African Countries [5]

Following the intention to investigate the already reported dismissive comments by a Conference Director*, that "the number of failed renewable energy projects in Africa over the last 20 years is unacceptable, and verging on the irresponsible," the failures and successes in Nigeria have been reviewed. It may be necessary to review power supply projects on renewable energy resources and their results in other African countries. It is relevant to examine the causes of failures or successes in order to encourage or discourage such investments.

World Bank Funding: Solar Power in Kenya [5]

The World Bank on 26 July 2017 approved an International Development Association (IDA) credit equivalent to $150 million to help fund delivery of modern energy services via off-grid solar in Kenya. The initiative has been described as the "Off-grid Solar Access Project for Underserved Counties."

---

* Name omitted deliberately.

It is expected to provide modern, off-grid solar electricity services to an estimated 1.3 million people in 277,000 households across 14 counties of Kenya.

Hon. Charles Keter, E.G.H, Kenya Cabinet Secretary for Energy and Petroleum, made the following comments on the project: "The Ministry appreciates this project which will go a long way in contributing to the achievement of one of the Government's objectives of attaining universal access to electrification by 2020."

The benefits of the project comprised the following:

- It entailed collaboration of public and private sectors.
- It consists of embedded operation and maintenance.
- It included an arrangement for financing the solar home system.
- It should help in accelerating off-grid electrification, which had been difficult to achieve.

Diarietou Gaye, World Bank Country Director for Kenya, had this to say:

> The World Bank is committed to supporting the growth of Kenya's under-served areas through linking homes, communities and the businesses that serve them to clean and renewable energy sources. By connecting 1.3 million people to off-grid solar energy, these counties can begin harnessing the fruits of devolution by opening avenues for creation of more businesses and job opportunities.

Local Solar Vendors and Distributors

In 2018, there were at least two main solar energy distributors in Kenya: D. Light and Mobisol. D. Light announced that in 2016, an average of 800 Kenyan households a day were signing up for its D30 Pay-Go solar home system.

Mobisol, the other mobile "pay as you go" off-grid solar home vendor in Kenya, on 17 March announced that it was opening 20 new retail solar outlets in Kenya.

Both D. Light and Mobisol offered a mixture of off-grid, mobile "pay as you go" home solar products and services packages. The packages consist of a basic home solar starter kits supplied with solar panels and a battery pack and a smart meter. They include such items as solar flashlights lanterns, lamps with built-in mobile device chargers and LED lighting to small DC home appliances, such as fans, radios, TVs and even refrigerators.

Mobile Pay-Go Solar Energy in Zambia Aims at 850,000 Homes [6]

On 2 August 2017, Telecoms multinational MTN announced it was extending its partnership with Fenix International, a leading vendor in Africa's off-grid mobile pay-go (PAYG) solar home systems, to Zambia. The funding was from Swedish Embassy of nearly $3 million from 2017 to 2020, and USAID contributing $750,000.

Fenix aimed to reach 850,000 Zambians in rural areas. "Over 90% of rural Zambians lack access to electricity and have no options other than dangerous candles and kerosene lanterns to light their homes," stated Fenix International CEO Lyndsay Handler. Fenix's ReadyPay Power product is a modular, scalable off-grid home solar energy system that customers pay for in as small as the equivalent of 20 US cents – over time via MTN's Mobile Money e-payments service, which is widespread across Zambia. Handler reportedly also said: "With MTN's distribution networks, we'll be able to reach unbanked and off-grid customers. Once power and credit are established, the possibilities to bring other life-changing products – from smart phones to financial services – are endless."

Ghana's Renewable Energy Project of Solar Photovoltaic (PV) and Wind Power Minigrids [7]

Five small-scale solar-wind and energy storage minigrids were built by the Ghana Energy Development and Access Project (GEDAP). Ghana is a country of some 27 million residents (median age 21), about 20% of the population lacks access to grid electricity and 46% of these are in rural areas.

The five-remote solar-wind plus energy storage minigrids were planned to provide emissions-free power and energy 24 hours a day, 7 days a week. This should lead to beneficial socioeconomic opportunities and to improve the quality of life of about 3,500 Ghanaians living in remote island communities on Ghana's Volta Lake. Ghana already had a plan to achieve universal electricity access by 2020.

Questions

1. Why were solar and other renewable energy sources used instead of grid electricity in many places discussed in this chapter?
2. Kindly list the areas of use and the benefits derived.
3. What are the advantages and disadvantages of renewable energy supply? Please note that one is limited in what one can use in a renewable energy supply. For example, one may not use an air conditioner unless the power capacity of the supply is high enough to accommodate such a load.
4. Kindly criticise the statement that the investment on renewable energy is a waste of money. Please give reasons for agreeing or disagreeing with it even as it should be noted that the essence of investment on any type of power supply is to achieve sustainable and stable supply.

References

1. Ben Black, Worldwatch Institute – vision for sustainable growth, "African renewable energy gains attention," 12 September 2008.
2. Mikkel Ostergaard/Panos, "Study breaks down Nigerian solar power failure"; Nigeria: study breaks down Nigerian solar power failure, published in all Africa, 19 January 2016. http://www.scidev.net/global/energy/news/nigerian-solar-power-failure.html
3. Bolanle Omisore, "Nigeria's solar projects yield both failure and success," written for *National Geographic News*, 3 November 2011.
4. Solar Power Nigeria, Abuja, Nigeria, info@solar-ng.com, www.solar-ng.com
5. Africa Microgrid News World Bank Spurs Kenya Off-Grid Solar Expansion with $150MM IDA Credit, Andrew Burger, 31 July 2017.
6. Andrew Burger, "Africa microgrid news: Mobile pay-go solar leader aims to reach 850,000 Zambians by 2020," 10th August 2017.
7. Andrew Burger, "Spain's TTA builds five 24/7 solar-wind minigrids on Ghana's lake Volta islands," *Microgrid News,* 26 July 2018.

SECTION 3

DEFINITION OF PROBLEMS, REVIEW AND SUGGESTIONS FOR SOLUTIONS

3

In this section, a definition of the problems is prepared. It comprises a comprehensive review of the problems discussed in the earlier chapters. The causes of failure of the projects represent the problems addressed for solution in this book.

From research, a number of causes and incidents of failures have been found such that it is necessary to group them since some of them occur in various forms and have similar solutions. These have been presented in the next three chapters.

They are considered important because they provide information on the ills and failings in our system. Reading these cases should help project team members and managers understand and prepare for what they may see when they get involved in projects in Africa and probably in some other countries. "Well begun is half the job" and "To be forewarned is to be forearmed" are statements relevant in trying to do project management, and to address the ills that beset project delivery.

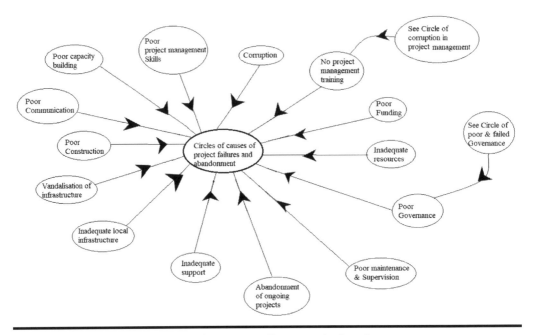

Figure S3.1   Circles of Causes of Project Failures and Abandonment.

To bring these problems into focus, Circles of Causes of Project Failures and Circles of Corruption in Project Management have been prepared so that they graphically present the problems at a glance on a page in each case. The figure for the Circles of Causes of Project Failures is displayed in this introduction to Section 3 (Figure S3.1), and the figures for Circles of Corruption in Project Management are given in Chapter 10 and the Circles of Poor Governance, in Chapter 11.

Chapter 9

Lack of Resources, Poor Planning and Poor Project Management

The various real-life examples discussed are summarised in this chapter, starting with poor planning.

Poor planning: Some of the instances that this occurred are given below:

1. **Too many projects with very limited funds:** This happens as a result of poor budgeting and starting more projects than the country can finance in order to fulfil unrealistic campaign promises. This was highlighted by a researcher in Ghana [1].

2. Poor planning was the main cause of the initial failures of renewable energy projects. It led to the following causes of failures [2, 3]:
   - There was no information to plan for the number of users.
   - The project team could not ascertain a suitable location for the solar parks.
   - There was no reliable arrangement for resources for the immediate and sustainable operation and maintenance of the delivered renewable energy supply.

3. It led to the failure to include the local community in planning, project implementation and operations of the project deliverables as shown in the following examples:
   - It was alleged that a Ghanaian local government failed to understand why members of a community were contracting a particular disease,

it assumed that providing a water borehole should help stop the disease in fulfilment of a manifesto promise. However, the community refused to use the provided borehole because of their traditional belief in the usage of water from the stream.

– In South Africa, there was poor planning and implementation in some of their projects according to the article: "South Africa: Why Have All the Rural Tech Projects Failed?" It was observed that nearly every government plan stated project deliverable at the end of 10, 20 and 40 years without discussing the implementation, monitoring and correction plans. It was alleged that there had been many funds but little knowledge of how to plan and invest it, this led to little achievement [4].

– Again, in South Africa, there was poor project management, especially incompetent requirements management in the planning and purchase of Nelson Mandela Bay Metropolitan Municipality Metro Buses.

– Poor financial management led to the failure of the Sentech's MyWireless in South Africa in 2010.

– Poor planning as shown in the failure to involve the community in installation, project management and failure in capacity building in the community, training and resources for immediate and sustainable operation and maintenance of boreholes.

A suggested solution and example of success: In South Arica, the excellent cooperation between Microsoft and the local communities as discussed on "Digital Villages" could be recommended as a solution to the problem of establishing cooperation and partnership between communities and foreign companies and even with local government organisations [4].

4. Failure to plan and arrange for the maintenance and operation of the project deliverables. Some examples include the following:

– Failure in financing the operations and maintenance of commissioned and taken-over project deliverables: An example was the failure of the steel projects in Nigeria. Global Steel Holding Limited (GSHL), an Indian company, was given concessions for the Ajaokuta Steel Company Limited in 2004 and the Delta Steel Company Limited in 2005 by President Obasanjo "to clear the outstanding workers' salaries and take up the running of the plant." The government could not manage some of the completed plant units. It was spending a lot of money to pay salaries of hundreds of workers who were producing no income [6].

Suggested solution: The problem was due to poor planning. It was a sad scenario that major national projects that involved the investments of billions of dollars were planned and implemented without any plan of how the project deliverables could be operated to yield incomes. These incomes were needed to keep the project deliverables in operation and also to provide revenue that should recoup the fund invested in the projects.

It was the case that generally our national development plans consisted of projections of expenditures over many years on various projects. The plans might not include estimates of expected revenue generations by the project deliverables after being commissioned and put into operations. It is doubtful whether there was any discussion on the return on investments on our national projects. Our national budgets may not be properly developed as business plans which could provide the basis for our national development plan. It is suggested that a national project management unit could be established with the features and characteristics of a corporate department of a large commercial organisation. It should prepare and develop its vision, mission, strategic objectives such that they should constitute the basis for the national plan which should be effective and functional as a commercial corporate business plan.

- **Failure to provide for long-term, lifecycle management and the sustainability of the designed life of the project deliverables:** Many infrastructure projects, such as those for electric power plants, are planned and executed without any sustainable plan of how to keep the project deliverables in operation over its planned lifetime after the project team has left the site. Consequently, we are saddled with the failure of the deliverables and the abandonment of projects.

Suggested solution: Projects in developing countries have to be planned, designed and executed to accommodate the deficiencies in infrastructure in the locality, and poor knowledge of project management of the recipient user organisations. Two issues need to be addressed in an effort to solve this problem. They are:

- Planning and providing resources for the sustainability of project deliverables.
- Organising for training and adequate knowledge transfer for operation and maintenance of the commissioned deliverables.

Planning and providing resources for sustainability: A shortcoming in our project management practice is the fact that only resources for the implementation of a new project are normally planned for. When the project is completed, resources for the operation and maintenance of the project deliverables may not be available because it is not likely that they have been planned and provided for.

To solve this recurrent and widespread unhelpful practice, a management system that considers the provision of resources for new projects and for the operation and maintenance of completed project deliverables should be installed. In project portfolio management lifecycle, for example, new projects and project deliverables which are used in operation are all considered and prioritised as items that should be invested with the organisation's limited resources. Using priority weightings as a guide, it may be decided that it is more strategically beneficial and rewarding to invest in the operation and maintenance of some project deliverables than on some new projects. In such considerations, resources are provided for the operation and maintenance of some project deliverables. It may then mean that, given the limited resources of the organisation, some new projects of lower priority are not implemented because there are no resources for their implementation.

Organising for training and adequate knowledge transfer for operation and maintenance:

Most of the failures were recorded as a result of lack of skills, poor planning and absence of project management training. Indeed, most failures are traceable to these causes. The fact had been that the project deliverables failed because the users had no clue of how to maintain and keep them in operation. It does stand to reason that a well-trained workman becomes a competent workman; otherwise, he will not have the knowledge to deliver on the job. Since in many cases, contractors who implement projects are from other companies, it is necessary that the staff of the project owner and user company should be trained during the implementation. Their training could be the first item in the implementation plan. With this, the trained staff could also join the contractors in the implementation. By the completion of the project, they may be knowledgeable about the new project deliverables.

According to the plan for human resource requirements for the company's operations, some of the staff are then trained on the operation and maintenance of the new equipment or the project deliverable. Following this, they could be given a free hand to operate and maintain the facility even before the contractors leave the project site. Within the period of warranty, the customer staff should have developed competence and confidence in the operation and maintenance of the equipment.

Training the staff is just one aspect of the responsibility; retaining the trained staff is another. It was sadly the case that because government conditions of service were generally uncompetitive compared with those of large multinationals, such as the oil companies, the trained staff were lured away and employed by the oil companies and other multinationals who paid them sometimes more than twice of what the government could pay. Therefore, it should be necessary that the trained staff should be placed on attractive salaries, augmented with other benefits that make their remuneration attractive. It might be advisable that a few more staff should be employed and trained to work along the trained staff. This could help to ensure that if some of the trained staff left, the company should not be grounded because of their exit as the newly trained staff could keep the company operational.

Failure to provide for sustainability of project deliverables: When any foreign aid service is being provided to a developing nation, for example, it is not encouraged to buy the equipment and drop it with the community and go home. No, that is a recipe for disaster. This is one of the main findings of this research. As Mr. Jamie Skinner wrote in the section on water:

> There is no point an external agency coming in, putting in a drill-hole and then passing it over to the local community if they can't afford to maintain it over the next 10 or 20 years. There needs to be a proper assessment of just how much local people are able to finance these water points. It's not enough to just drill and walk away.

This author completely agrees with this view which is borne of his years of operations in developing nations.

In the past 60 or more years from 2018, projects of the then ultra-modern power stations and steel plants, among other industrial facilities, have been implemented, commissioned and put into operations. Following failure of parts which could not be procured, especially plant electronics, control and automation systems and equipment, it became impossible to keep some production and ancillary plants in operation. This contributed to the abandonment of many commissioned industrial plants just three to four years after being put into operation. Some examples include the following:

A Nigerian government commissioned audit revealed that 11,886 Federal Government projects failed in 40 years up to 2011 (i.e. about 300 projects failed every year), with the attendant loss of billions of dollars. In October 2016, a former Director-General of the Bureau of Public Procurement stated that there were 19,000 Federal Government projects in various stages of abandonment.

Suggested solution: A probable reason for failure could be the absence of project management office to provide appropriate practice of project management and sustainability. As already stated, it is sad that currently, up to 2019 when this book was prepared, most federal ministers and some governors discuss new projects without the involvement of relevant Nigerian professionals. No one person is professionally qualified to discuss the various aspects of a new project such as engineering, financial, legal, etc., on behalf of a country. This is why in developed countries, there are national and government project management offices and agencies staffed with appropriate professionals with expertise in various technical specialities who have responsibilities for both short and long-term national projects. Such professionals participate in project negotiation. They also plan for the long-term sustainability of major projects in the nation. In the UK, for example, they have the Infrastructure and Projects Authority (IPA). The way forward, as already suggested, should be to establish a National Project Management Office (NPMO) charged with the responsibility of end-to-end project management in the country. A short write-up on a National Project Management Office (NPMO) is contained in Appendix 1.

Community/user involvement: Research shows that where the communities are involved in projects from the start, with their operatives trained and resources provided for the operation of the taken-over project deliverables, success is recorded. The Microsoft business plan for the South African Digital Village, the AMREF operated boreholes and the SELF-operated solar power plants in Jigawa, Nigeria, discussed earlier in this book, are all success stories because the local communities were involved in the planning, participated in the project, involved in the operation and provided with sustained resources for the operation of the deliverable after takeover.

Questions

1. List examples in which projects failed because of poor planning.
2. Suggest actions that could be taken to prevent such failures.
3. Some projects fail because they could not be maintained and sustained in operations after the deliverables were taken over by the owners/users. Please suggest causes of the failures.
4. How can such causes be prevented as lessons learned in a new project?

References

1. I. S. Damoh, "An investigation into the causes and effects of project failure in government projects in developing countries: Ghana as a case study Isaac Sakyi Damoah," A thesis submitted in partial fulfilment of the requirements of Liverpool John Moores University for the degree of Doctor of Philosophy, October 2015.
2. Mikkel Ostergaard/Panos, "Study breaks down Nigerian solar power failure"; Nigeria: study breaks down Nigerian solar power failure, published in all Africa, 19 January 2016. http://www.scidev.net/global/energy/news/nigerian-solar-power-failure.html.
3. Bolanle Omisore, "Nigeria's solar projects yield both failure and success," *National Geographic News*, 3 November 2011.
4. Kathryn Cave, "South Africa: why have all the rural tech projects failed?" Editor, IDG Connect, 21 June 2013.
5. "Digital villages," https://www.microsoft.com/southafrica/community/digital.htm
6. Ajibola Amzat, "How Nigerian government, Indians wreck multi-billion dollar Delta Steel Company, rip off host communities and tax payers," 12 February 2018, https://guardian.ng/features/how-nigerian-government-indians-wreck-multi-billion-dollar-delta-steel-company-rip-off-host-communities-and-tax-payers/

Chapter 10

Problems of Corruption, Zero Productivity and Poor Return on Investment

In this chapter, some examples of the problems of corruption are presented.

1. **Public enterprise projects in Nigeria:** As discussed already in Chapter 2, the Director-General* of Bureau of Public Enterprise (BPE), from 1999 to 2003 in Nigeria, explained that from 1970 to 1999 the Federal Government invested over $100 billion in establishing public enterprises but earned only 0.5% return on investment. He said that the companies were costing the government about $2.65 billion annually to maintain. According to him,

   the late 1970s was a period that public enterprises were not working instead they were not only a drain on the economy, they were not providing services and not solving the problem they were meant to solve but were captured by the elites for their own benefits.

   Suggested solution: Corruption, as discovered in this research, in its many forms, is widespread in all the nations on which our research has been conducted: Nigeria, South Africa and Ghana. Corruption is a problem that has to be resolved, and plans are made for its elimination whenever projects are being undertaken in an African country. This could be true in other developing countries. It

---

* Name deliberately omitted.

constitutes over 60% of the causes of failures of the projects based on the information collated from the research for this book. It is not confined to one country; rather, it exists in African countries, and also occurs internationally. The research shows that it is encountered at every stage of the project lifecycle. Actually, in some cases, it may even predate the project because the practice of bribery and corruption starts even before the contract is awarded. It occurs during planning and requirements preparation and management, as bribes are paid to redefine the scope of the project. It occurs during execution, monitoring and closing. Payments and sign-off for job completion are also influenced by corruption as contractors may be paid for uncompleted work and also paid more than the agreed sum as the government officials arrange to receive their shares of the fraudulent payments from the contractors.

It appears difficult to suggest a solution because whatever is suggested will be implemented by persons. If they are not won over in the fight against corruption, the solution may not be successful because those implementing it will look for loopholes in the solution to exploit.

In spite of this discouraging and negative assessment, corruption should be seen as an enterprise risk and its solution should be considered in the preparation and installation of an enterprise risk management system in the organisation.

It is important that there should be people who are committed to the eradication of corruption. For any system to deliver the desired result, it has been observed that "[m]ethodologies and processes don't deliver [programmes and] projects; people do" (PwC). And, "if an organization is to undertake all the [programmes and] projects necessary to implement the chosen organizational strategy, there must be sufficient people with the right competences, skills, attitudes, and know-how to deliver the full portfolio." This writer has a first-hand experience of the truth of this statement. In 2007, he was making a presentation on the benefits of a project management product from Primavera Systems Incorporated to a company in Lagos, Nigeria. To his shock, he discovered that two or three persons in his audience were busy trying to discover loopholes in the management of the project which they could exploit to falsify project data. He could not but stop to advise them that basic honesty is required in data collection and for systems to work correctly.

2. **Failure to Complete the Complex Nuclear Technology Centre Worth about $52 million in 2012 Because of Alleged Corruption, Mismanagement and Lack of Fund and Poor Project Management**

    Suggested solution: The poor organisation of the project management system contributes mainly to this problem. It is here suggested that the proper approach could be as follows:
    - For example, with a project portfolio management system, given a limited amount of fund, there should be a choice of selected and prioritised number and types of projects.
    - The choice is made such that the available fund can be used for the complete implementation of the projects and also to provide for the operation and maintenance of the project deliverables.
    - A plan for implementation of the projects and also the disbursement of the fund for the implementation is made and approved with the necessary contingencies to attend to unforeseen problems that may arise.
    - Timeline for implementation of the project should be prepared and implemented.

    With this implementation, projects are completed as planned. Therefore, the issue of lack of fund to complete a project is indicative of the poor project management system. The problem of corruption has been discussed and suggestions have been made on how to fight it and try to eliminate it. The introduction of enterprise risk management and training of staff on the long-term benefits of eliminating corruption in the system are the procedures suggested.

3. **Failure to maintain public refineries because of alleged corruption:** Nigeria, a major producer of oil, is the world's largest importer of fuel because of very low outputs from the four Nigerian refineries. They are functioning poorly because of lack of overhaul maintenance for over 10 years. Contracts awarded for their repairs were either abandoned halfway or not executed at all as a result of alleged corruption and embezzlement of voted funds.

    Suggested solution: From the research carried out for this publication, it was discovered that corruption had been institutionalised in a number of large public offices in many African countries. As a result, allowing organisations to continue their operations without any external checks will be unhelpful as the practice of corruption is already endemic in the culture of the organisation. Therefore, interventions by a project management office are essential in the fight to eradicate corruption. Adaptive monitoring and project auditing could be conducted by the PMO to check the activities of project teams and even maintenance office. Such checks could help to show how resources and funds are being utilised. The checks could be planned or interventionist to provide information on the use of resources. Based on the findings, corrective actions should follow to correct the ills discovered. All these suggested actions should be components of the Enterprise Risk Management (ERM) framework. The framework is discussed in Appendix 9.

However, as has often been the case in Africa, interference by government ministries contributes a lot to the corruption. It is a problem of governance which the PMO cannot eliminate. It is the government that has to impose discipline in the operations of the ministries and anti-corruption measures to stop the unacceptable interference.

4. **Corruption through lack of accountability:** There were instances where a state official was the chairperson of a government project and was also the sole supplier of materials for the project at a rate which was above the market rate for the same project. In these cases, the supplier of materials for the projects was the same government official who awarded the contract. In effect, the contractor and the government official could be the same person or another who colluded with the official to inflate the prices and then share the excess as their ill-gotten "profits."

   Suggested Solution: This example is just one of many which occur because of the use of a poor project management system and could be resolved with the use of Enterprise Project Management. As discussed in the last section, the use of the strategic PMO and PPM makes for effective governance. Good governance will help to eliminate corruption in the system, indiscipline and lack of accountability. It is discussed in the next chapter.

5. **Corruption – delay in payment attracts bribes from contractors to speed up their payments:** This delay is in the bureaucratic procedure in government project implementation and numerous channels that contractors have to go through to obtain their payments. In order to cut down on the delay, they do a "follow up" by giving bribes to "speed up the payment" process. In effect, the slow pace of the government payment process constrains contractors to pay bribes in return for quick payment.

6. **10% payment to win a contract:** Contractors report the payment of 10% of the contract money to government officials. It is alleged that it is "extremely difficult or impossible" for a contractor to win a contract if the money is not paid.

7. **Unofficial middlemen and lack of contract work supervision:** Unofficial and unauthorised middlemen serve as the "link" between the contractor and the public servant. It is alleged that "[r]arely would you be able to win a contract if you do not have such middlemen who can connect you." They are fronts to government officers and charge both the contractor and the government officials for their services, the charges are added onto the contract sum. Following the deal, the winner of the contract is agreed even before the official bidding.

   The other damage done by this corruption is that the government officials are unable to supervise the project effectively and enforce compliance with work specifications because they have compromised their authority by the corrupt and illegal arrangement with the contractor.

8. **Corruption: Refusal to Monitor and Inspect Project without Payment of "Fuel Costs"**

   Some government consultants and officers often fail to inspect projects if contractors fail to bribe them by paying unofficial "fuel costs" to enable them to visit the project site for inspection. For example, they would not approve documentation for contractors who do not pay, or sign their documents, and even abandon projects. This was seen as one of the problems in Ghana and probably in other countries.

9. **Corruption in government tender for contract award:** There was corruption reported in the award of contracts in South Africa as already discussed in Section 2, Chapter 5. Moreover, it was alleged that some tenders were disqualified for "insignificant reasons" as government officials manipulated tenders to suit their purposes.

   Suggested solution: This is another form of corruption which could be resolved using suggestions made for standard illegal payments in the construction industry in South Africa. One had to pay public officials for the contract (work), pay for the processing of payments, pay for meetings. The payments start "at the top of most organizations and the amounts decreased in descending positions of the individuals."

   On their own part, public officials deliberately overpaid favoured contractors irrespective of the figures in the official payment certificate because, as already explained, they shared the overpayment as part of their "profit" with the contractors.

10. **Zero productivity with regular payment of full salary in the failed Nigerian steel industry:** As a result of indiscipline and gross inefficiency, the concept of working for the government as practised in some African countries, especially Nigeria, was that when one reported to the office daily, one expected to be paid. It was not a concern whether or not any income was generated. The thinking was that the very act of reporting to work should attract a salary.

Suggested solution: As already explained, our public enterprises in Africa appear to be generally operated without any planned forecast of income generation. A government electricity generation plant, for example, or a steel production plant, a petroleum refinery or any other government industrial plant is planned, commissioned and put in operation. The emphasis is to keep it in operation without any downtime. There is hardly any serious consideration for the income being generated. What is the efficiency of our operation? What is our productivity? These questions do not appear on the table for discussion. There is no arrangement to ensure that the revenue generated can be adequate to fund the operations of the plant which include salaries, cost of raw materials, cost of spare parts, cost of maintenance and replacement, etc.

To expatiate, this author was a chief engineer in a steel plant, it was not unusual to hear at the regular weekly Monday morning company-wide production meeting that the steel rods produced a day or two earlier had failed the quality control test. They were therefore downgraded to scrap which could not be sold to customers but returned to the furnace for reheating. In effect, the cost of materials, cost of fuel and cost of thousands of man-hours invested in their production were lost. It was during his MBA programme at the University of Bradford, UK, in a course on quality management that he learnt that quality cannot be inspected into a product. Rather to ensure that a product meets the desired quality specifications, quality has to be built into it right from the raw materials and throughout the production process and equipment using quality management processes. He shuddered as he recalled the large amount of losses they were incurring as they often downgraded products, made after several hours of large-scale operations, to scrap.

As a result of this mode of operations, the steel company owed other government departments a large debt for the costs of gas and electricity which they could not pay. When the gas and electricity

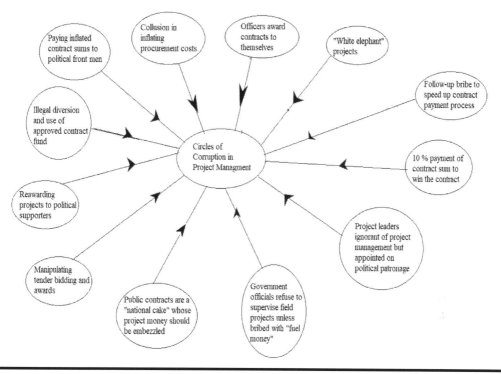

Figure 10.1   Circles of corruption in project management.

supplies were cut off, the minister in charge appealed to the respective ministers to advise their departments to restore them. This is not an indictment on his company; in any case, it was a universal practice in public companies. Rather it is highlighting the fact that government enterprises have to be operated with the discipline of the market and some knowledge of business management. It is the same indiscipline and lack of knowledge that account for people being paid without revenue being generated in their operation as discussed earlier. The Nigerian steel companies collapsed because of lack of fund. The same was true for other government companies which had no plans to generate income to keep them in operation but depended on funds from the government.

Summary

The figure of circles of corruption in project management graphically contains the causes of corruption discussed in the chapter (Figure 10.1).

Questions

    i. List at least five corrupt practices discussed in the chapter.

   ii. Have you observed any of them in any organisation?

  iii. Now that you know about them, please suggest how they can be avoided in your organisation.

Chapter 11

Failed Governance, Majorly Contributory to Failed Projects in Africa

A lot of the failed major projects in Africa belong to the public sector and are owned by the various national governments. Multinationals such as Shell, Chevron, Total, Agip, etc., plan and implement projects but do not experience the failures that occur in government-owned projects, at least not at a comparable rate.

For example, in 1980–1981, as a young professional, the writer worked in Shell Warri in Nigeria. He observed a new set of gas turbine electric generators being installed to replace the diesel generators in operation. The explanation was that the diesel generators would no longer be supported after a few years, it was therefore essential to build the turbine generators which could be sustained for many years in the future.

This was an example of the forward thinking and planning required of good governance.

Governance defines processes undertaken by a government or a board of directors and other such bodies to direct management or the body being governed to conduct actions or policies for the achievement of the desired objectives of the nation or organisation. In effect, the board in case of commercial organisations, or national executive council for governments, authorises and delegates the respective executive management of Federal Government parastatals, organisations or companies the power to carry out programmes, projects and operations. Members of the executive or top management of the government organisations are appointed by the government. They are responsible to the government and can be sacked or redeployed as the relevant government minister decides.

This arrangement underscores the need to investigate the contributions of the actions or inactions of government ministers and their representatives in the failure and abandonment of projects.

The following topics will be investigated and analysed:

■ Governance as it relates to government ministries and government parastatals and companies
■ Examples of actions or inactions of government ministries
■ Failed governance, a symptom of a corrupt and failed democracy
■ Suggestions on how to correct the flaws in the present arrangement in order to achieve successful and sustainable project delivery
■ Concluding remarks

Most of this information is based on the experience of the writer or taken from research papers published after a real-life survey of people who had worked in public organisations in their respective African countries. The analysis is started with the first topic.

1. **Governance as it relates to government ministries and government parastatals and companies**

Appointments in parastatals are based on political inclination. Some of the interviewed persons described the roles of the boards to include the following:
  – Formulation of policies for parastatals and government organisations
  – Appointment of members of the board and of the top management
  – Approving the promotion of staff
  – Considering and approving budgets of parastatals
  – Awarding contracts
  – Approving the disciplines of staff
  – Generally, regulating the activities of parastatals
In effect, the board, by the above roles, governs parastatals.
Governance as defined by one of the interviewed persons is: "a process of administering organisations, people or society using the resources available to ensure that the resources are properly invested." Or simply put "administering people and resources to achieve certain results."

Quality of Members Appointed to the Board [1]

The members of parastatals governing boards are appointed by the government of the day. However, all the interviewed persons declared that:

1. "The appointments of members of parastatals governing boards are politically motivated."
2. "Their appointments are based on political patronage, tribal sentiment, religious bigotry, ethnic balancing, party strongman, and political rewards for their active participation in political campaigns."

For example, an interviewee argued: "It is a political patronage. It is a winner takes all. You cannot be appointed into a board without being a party member. It is not based on merit. It is based on ethnic, religious and party considerations."

Another interviewed person, who was a former head of a parastatal, explained:

> The appointment of members of boards is politically motivated. You must be a party strongman before you are appointed to a position in a parastatal.
>
> All board members are political appointees. The appointment is used to compensate them for campaigning for their master. How do you think they will perform? They are there to serve their godfathers who recommended them to that position and to make returns to them.

Two other interviewed persons "contended that, there is a complete disregard for integrity, character, professional competence and qualification, values, years of experience, and track records of antecedents of the person being appointed."

They confirmed that "the appointments of the chief executive of parastatals are politically motivated; based on political party or on ethnic balancing."

Another interviewed person contended that "the appointment of chief executives of parastatals is not based on merit but on ethnic balancing and at the discretion of the President or a State Governor."

Comparison with Successful Parastatals Overseas [2]

It is observed that success achieved by parastatals in Singapore, for example, could be traced to capabilities of the board. It is reported that:

- "The best person (is given) the job, notwithstanding the person's background and nationality."
- There are "high calibre of people on the board and the strength of people in-charge of parastatals."
- The Singaporean government has been able to achieve this success through Temasek Holdings Limited (THL). It is owned by the government and yet independent of government control. THL supervises Singaporean parastatals and helps them to succeed in order to maximise social benefits for the Singaporean nation.

  The following information on their operations strategy is published in the 2017 Annual Review for Temasek Holdings Limited (THL):

  Temasek is an investment company. We own and manage our assets based on commercial principles.

  As an active investor, we shape our portfolio by increasing, holding or decreasing our investment holdings. These actions are driven by a set of commercial principles to create and maximise risk-adjusted returns over the long term.

  As an engaged shareholder, we promote sound corporate governance in our portfolio companies. This includes the formation of high calibre, experienced and diverse boards.

  Our portfolio companies are guided and managed by their respective boards and management; we do not direct their business decisions or operations.

  Similarly, our investment, divestment and other business decisions are directed by our board and management. Neither the President of Singapore nor our shareholder, the Singapore Government, is involved in our business decisions.

2. **Examples of actions or inactions of government ministries**
   - **Interference in operations:** Interference by government officials in the production operations of a steel company in Nigeria. An ex-general manager disclosed in a press interview how government officials terminated a contract of a supplier who was supplying raw materials at N600 (about $4.00) per ton and replaced him with another who supplied the same quality of material at N1000 (about $7.00) per ton [3].
   - **Lack of accountability:** The structure of corporate governance with accountability is centred on the boards, managers and the shareholders. Sadly, the performances of the various government

large public organisations reveal a lack of transparency and account-ability. For example, there was the allegation of fraud perpetuated by some past Managing Directors of the Nigerian National Petroleum Corporation. It was reported that some of them were involved in the Halliburton and Willbros bribery scandals. A case in point was that one of them was reportedly caught red-handed with $2 million cash which he was unable to account for; another was said to have appro-priated the sum of $17 million meant for the turn-around mainte-nance of the Kaduna Refinery. In addition, the Managing Directors were said to have formed the habit of not remitting proceeds realised from the sale of Nigeria crude oil to the federation account [4].

- Two writers, Sarbah and Wen (2014), disclosed that in Ghana, "the roots of parastatals' failure are: excessive intervention; corrup-tion; the CEO taking decisions following ministerial instructions or approval; and the board chair overriding the CEO on operational decisions." Another author (Odhiambo-Mbai, 2003) wrote that "in Kenya immediately after independence parastatals were found char-acterised by nepotism, ethnicity, and appointments and promotions were not based on the principle of meritocracy."

- An author, Maduagwu (1982), wrote that "in Nigeria, any govern-ment official or politician … in a position to enrich himself cor-ruptly but [failing] to do so will … be ostracised by his people upon leaving office. He would be regarded as a fool, or selfish, or both." "Appointments into positions and offices are to be used to benefit people from their primordial public (their own select public group) and seen as a way of sharing in the 'national cake' or national resources" [5].

- Government ineptitude, incompetence and indiscipline contributed majorly to the failure and abandonment of the steel industry for many years.

The steel industry was started by Alhaji Shehu Shagari, the Prime Minister of Nigeria from 1979 to 1983. He had Ajaokuta Steel Company Limited (ASCL) as a direct responsibility of his office and was so interested that he visited it regularly. He was overthrown in a military coup on 31 December 1983. Sadly, they did not pay much attention to ASCL, except completing the already planned administration block.

A panel in 1994 discovered that between 1988 and 1994, a dedicated and special account with the Central Bank of Nigeria (CBN) amounting to $12.4

billion was depleted to $200 million in June 1994 (Apter 2005; Agbiboa, 2012). The fund was for three major special development projects which were the Shiroro Hydro-Electricity project, ASCL and National Iron Ore Mining Company (NIOMCO), Itakpe. The Military President, General Ibrahim Babangida, explained that the $12.4 billion meant for ASCL and others was not stolen but used for "regenerative investment and critical infrastructure" such as the building of Abuja City and Lagos Third Mainland Bridge (Daniel, 2015). The fact of the matter was that fund earmarked for work on the steel industry was allegedly diverted and used in other projects. Worse was to come in the dissolution of the NSDA.

Dissolution of the Nigeria Steel Development Authority (NSDA)

The NSDA was established in 1971 on the advice of the Russians who were building the Ajaokuta Steel Company Limited (ASCL). The duties of the NSDA included the following:

- To plan, construct and operate the steel plants.
- To carry out geological surveys, study market, metallurgical research and train the staff.
- It was an agency staffed with Nigerian experts who could have professionally managed the steel industry.
- NSDA was similar to Temasek Holdings Limited (THL) owned by Singaporean Government. It was to do for Nigeria what THL had been doing for Singapore.

NSDA was dissolved in 1979 and their duties were taken over by the Ministry of Mines and Steel Development. Some of the interviewed persons reported that in the ministry, "a lot of activities were then haphazardly embarked upon; lots of inflated subsidiary projects were being simultaneously chased" (Anwar and Sam, 2006).

Lack of Continuity and Consistency in Successive Government Policies

In a country, there should be consistency and continuity in governance; there should be a system that continued from government to government.

However, the spate of project abandonment in some African countries when a new political party comes into government is alarming. As stated earlier in this book, there were about 11,886 neglected projects in Nigeria according to the reports of the Presidential Projects Assessment Committee (PPAC) set up in March 2011, by President Goodluck Jonathan to look into the cases of neglected Federal Government projects in Nigeria since independence in 1960 (EL-Rufai, 2012). This is a reflection of lack of consistency, lack of patriotism or lack of commitment to achieve a goal started by the previous administration.

According to one of the interviewed persons:

> [A] new government may not like to continue or improve on what the previous government did. Rather, what a new government used to do is to neglect the policies and projects initiated by the previous government and start its own projects. There will be no benefit accruing to a government that completes an old project.

Another interviewed person explained:

> The new government's attention will be drawn away from the old projects since kickbacks cannot be given from the old projects if they are to be continued by the new government. The old projects can only continue if they can be re-awarded and the new government can be assured of getting kickbacks.

Other reasons include the following:

> Another reason for neglecting projects as the possibility of relocating the project in their ethnic origin by the new leaders in order that the contract for the project to be re-awarded to their relations, children, friends or classmates.
>
> El-Rufai (2012), Olalusi and Otunola (2012) and Ubani and Ononuju (2013) include other reasons for neglecting projects as: "non continuation of policies and priorities as occupiers of political offices change; nepotism; corruption; re-awarding of projects to political supporters as generous campaign gifts at inflated prices; paying contract sum to political bigwigs; etc."

Lack of fund due to withholding of budget allocated fund: It is reported that money allocated in the budget may not be released to parastatal as when due. For example, one of the interviewed persons, who was a head of a parastatal and a chairman of a board of parastatal at the time of the interview, explained:

> The major problem of parastatals is that they are not financially autonomous. It is when you request for money before you get it even when it was allocated to the parastatal in the budget. It takes political manoeuvring to get what you want as a head of a parastatal. There is no deliberate attempt to release the money allocated to them in the budget.

Moreover,

> if any fund is released from the ministry, the Ministry of Mines and Steel Development will send a list of contractors to whom the job must be given; and it should not be given to any other contractor other than the ones the organisation was directed to give the job to otherwise the management will lose its job for incompetence.

Problem of Accountability

The 1999 Nigerian Constitution (as amended) mandates the National Assembly to monitor parastatals for the purpose of accountability. However, accountability to the National Assembly is reportedly flawed with fradulence. For example, a committee of the Nigerian House of Representatives on capital market headed by Representative R (name deliberately withheld) was being accused of corruption. The committee was investigating the reason for the near collapse of the capital market when it was accused of demanding for a bribe amounting to N44 million (about $300,000) from the Director-General of the Securities and Exchange Commission (SEC). The Director-General of SEC argued:

> Representative R is corrupt and lacks credibility. For instance, he collected estacode and other travel allowances from Securities and Exchange Commission (SEC) to travel to the Dominican Republic on a capacity enhancement conference for capital market regulators. He did not go neither did he return the money collected. Also, he asked the commission to contribute N39 million towards the

on-going charade of a public hearing and demanded another N5 million cash on Tuesday, March 13, 2012. He made both demands by proxy [6].

The Nigerian constitution empowers the National Assembly to investigate and expose corruption, but it is the same National Assembly committee that was supposed to expose corruption that was reportedly demanding bribes. Sadly, this is just one of many cases. Such incidents make accountability difficult.

3. Failed Governance, a Symptom of a Corrupt and Failed Democracy

From research, a long list of failures has been obtained that characterise the operations of African government ministries who have responsibilities for public organisations conducting projects. The failures include the following:

- Failure to continue projects started by the previous government.
- Nepotism, corruption, re-awarding of projects to political supporters as generous campaign gifts at inflated prices.
- Paying inflated contract sum to political bigwigs.
- Appointments of members of parastatals governing boards are politically motivated based on political patronage, party strongmen and political rewards for their active participation in political campaigns.
- Appointments based on tribal sentiment, religious bigotry and ethnic balancing.
- Appointees serve their godfathers who recommended them to that position and make financial returns and payments to them.
- Complete disregard for integrity, character, professional competence and qualification, values, years of experience and track records of antecedents of the person being appointed.

Actually, this should not be surprising because it was not feasible and realistic to expect that the members of boards of public parastatals and government companies could constitute an "island" of impeccable honesty and integrity in the country while the rest of the government functionaries including members of parliament, national assemblies and presidency were all corrupt. In spite of all the press coverage, even by the press of Western World, addressing some Nigerian leaders, even the current leaders in 2018, as honest and waging anti-corruption battles; the reality was completely different. As one contributor puts it, they were being addressed in "borrowed robes." Therefore, our attempt at running successful and disciplined democratic government for the interest of all nationals has so far failed as in 2019, at least, when this book was being published.

Little or No Accountability by Top Functionaries and Engaging in "White Elephant Projects"

It has been the practice for many years, especially since after the Nigerian Civil War, from 1971 to the present year, 2019, that top functionaries in African countries, for example, Nigeria, such as state governors, federal ministers, etc., have managed their responsibilities with little or no accountability. As a result, they have spent fund on "white elephant" projects. As already explained, a white elephant project could be described as one which is costly to maintain, and its cost is very high for its low value.

Suggested solutions: They include the suggestions discussed in the subsequent paragraphs, starting with the creation of a PMO.

4. Creation of a National Project Management Office (PMO)

The creation of a national project management office has been suggested as one of the solutions in this book. The PMO should have the right to check on projects including state government projects. A situation in which a public officer discusses the implementation and cost of a project without a third independent party involved gives the officer a free hand to agree on terms which may not be the best for the state. Investing state fund on projects with little value as already discussed is such an example. The right to decide and conclude transactions on new projects should belong to a PMO or such a nationally appointed body comprised of experts and professionals but not to a single person. This is further discussed in the next problem.

Failure of governance led to the failure of the Ghana-STX Building Project, a $10 billion housing project: Disunity and quarrels were reported between the Ghanaian and Korean partners of STX Engineering & Construction Ghana Limited, the local subsidiary of STX Korea.

Suggested solution: The absence of a nationally established and empowered project management unit with control over national projects accounts for absence of effective governance. The use of a national project management office (NPMO) and a project portfolio management (PPM), as already suggested, should ensure that there is an effective governance in an organisation.

For example, Strategic PMO ensures that all of the programmes and projects are carried out in an effective and efficient manner. It prevents any confusion, lack of accountability and poor coordination as the Strategic PMO helps to enhance governance and accountability. In addition, a successful project portfolio management strategy must comprise an end-to-end framework that guides an organisation from project selection through execution to commercial operation. An essential element of the framework is the PPM Governance. PPM Governance ensures the competent use of resources for enabling an organisation to achieve its goals. It has been said that a good governance structure is central to making PPM work. "Portfolio management without governance is an empty concept" [7].

Poor governance – incompetent leadership: Persons without knowledge of project management are appointed to project leadership because of their positions in the party or company.

Suggested solution: There could be two issues involved in this problem. The first is corruption. Appointing a person because of their position in a political party to lead a public infrastructure project is corruption. However, appointing someone without the knowledge of project management because of their position in the organisation and that the project falls within their responsibility is not corruption. It is poor planning and poor project management. It is necessary that the person is trained in order to be competent and confident to discharge their responsibility effectively. Nevertheless, these are some shortcomings that professionals and technocrats in developing countries have been experiencing. A cause of these is the absence of opportunities and facilities for training and even continual professional development.

It is often the case that a Permanent Secretary or a Director-General in a ministry is a graduate of first degree in history or even English, acquired some 20 or more years earlier. The person has risen by dint of hard work to become the head of the ministry. There is no local professional organisation in which they can update their skills. There is therefore the need for training in fundamentals of project management to give the person some grounding on the entailments of project management before they are given the responsibility of being a Director or final decision maker in a project worth millions of dollars. It stands to reason that one cannot be approving what one does not understand. Even when contractors bid for the project, the untrained and uninformed Director does not have the knowledge to assess their technical suitability to carry out the project. It is therefore not surprising that some projects cannot be supervised but are abandoned without

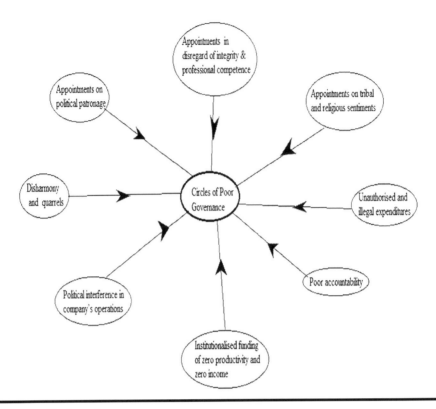

Figure 11.1   Circles of poor governance.

completion and the project money completely spent. Of course, using up the fund with the project abandoned borders on corruption.

A basic course on project management fundamentals, comprising definitions of frequently used words and terms, is suggested in Appendix 2. Doing this or a similar course could be helpful. It is entitled: "Project Management Fundamentals for Busy Executives and Managers in Developing Countries."

It should also be observed that with the proliferation of the Internet, any officer who wishes to update their knowledge and skill base may find appropriate courses online. However, older generation officers in developing countries have to learn to use such facilities because they may not even know how to use them (Figure 11.1).

5. Chapter Concluding Commentary

Most of our national governments have been corrupt for many years since the independence of our respective African governments. So long also have there been project failures and abandonment in the various countries. The surprise is that we have failed to associate the project failures to the failure of governance which derives from the failures, ineptitude and corruption of our national governments.

It has been sadly the case that any and every failure is blamed on the general and technical management of the government companies, especially the engineers. They are accused of poor technical skills, poor knowledge of project management, etc. These accusations still continue even in cases when world-class technical management and engineers from developed nations are involved. An example was the ultra-modern direct-reduction steel complex that was the Delta Steel Company, Aladja. As a chief engineer, this writer worked with technical assistants and consultants from a consortium of German and Austrian firms. Yet it also failed after a few years; the operations could not be sustained because, in the main, there was no arrangement for its independent financial operations and sustainability such that it could earn adequate income on its own. The interference of ministry officials in the operation of contractors has been reported earlier in this book. Again, this was one of many such cases. Failure in governance is a major contributory to the failure of these public companies. With all the best of intentions in the world, the engineers, including the Germans and Australia, could not have gone to the ministry to advise on how to resolve the problems in the plants caused by their corrupt practices and poor governance. There was no such arrangement.

Way Forward

From the reports, it is obvious that it is the corruption in the government that is carried over to the boards of parastatals leading to failure in governance. It is unrealistic waiting for the day when corruption will be eradicated in our nations or controlled to the point that it does not interfere with our national operations and projects. What is more realistic is to learn from the private sector companies who operate successfully in our nations.

It is clearly the case that public organisations should be made independent of government control. One of the differences between successful private companies and public companies is independence and freedom from government control. Their boards are appointed by shareholders who are stakeholders and not by politicians who have no stake in the companies. An example of such a successful arrangement of a government organisation being completely free from government control is the Temasek Holdings Limited (THL) of Singapore.

This therefore is a suggestion to international donors and aid companies who operate in Africa. It is to seek to ensure that the local companies which you intend to use are free from control of politicians and the government. This should help guarantee that there will be discipline, honesty and integrity in their governance which will majorly determine the success or failure of the projects and your investments.

Questions

- Please list the various manifestations of corruption in government organisations discussed in this section.
- List suggestions for their elimination.
- Have you had any personal experience of the impact of corruption in official transaction? How do you suggest that it could be eradicated?
- Please suggest other reasons for project failures discussed in this section.

References

1. Johnson Obera, "Governance and accountability issues in Nigerian parastatals: The case of Ajaokuta Steel," Doctor of Philosophy, University of Dundee.
2. 2017 Annual Review for Temasek Holdings Limited (THL) Singapore; Temasek International Pte. Ltd., Singapore. https://www.temasek.com.sg/en
3. Ajibola Amzat, "How Nigerian government, Indians wreck multi-billion dollar Delta Steel Company, rip off host communities and tax payers," 12 February 2018, https://guardian.ng/features/how-nigerian-government-indians-wreck-multi-billion-dollar-delta-steel-company-rip-off-host-communities-and-tax-payers/
4. I Ibrahim, the Plundering of N.N.P.C. Lagos, *Newswatch Magazine*, 19 April 2010.
5. Daniel Egiegba Agbiboa, "The corruption-underdevelopment nexus in Africa: which way Nigeria?!", *The Journal of Social, Political and Economic Studies*, Vol. 35, No. 4, 22 December 2010.

6. Ben Agande and Michael Eboh, "Capital market stabilization: reps asked me for N44m bribe – Oteh," 16 March 2012, 3:48 AMIN Headlines by VANGUARD, https://www.vanguardngr.com/2012/03/capital-market-stabilization-reps-asked-me-for-n44m-bribe-oteh/
7. Project Portfolio Governance Guidelines (But are they complete?) By R. Max Wideman, 2005, http://www.maxwideman.com/papers/governance/governance.pdf

SECTION 4
A FRAMEWORK FOR SUCCESSFUL MANAGEMENT OF PROJECTS, PROGRAMMES, AND PORTFOLIOS USING OPM, PPM LIFECYCLE & PMO

4

This section discusses a framework consisting of suggested processes for developing portfolios, programmes, and projects necessary for the successful selection and implementation of projects and the handover of project deliverables and their operations and maintenance.

The objectives of using the framework are as follows:

■ To suggest how a company should be so structured that it can be financially independent. It will not depend on a government or an external organisation for funding for its operations at the completion of the project.

- To present guidelines, processes, and procedures to minimise failures of projects and their deliverables.
- To provide information on how to enhance the achievement of sustainable and commercially competitive project deliverables.
- To discuss how to engage in financially profitable activities that should earn profits for their owners and stakeholders.

Learning Objective: To enable readers to understand the philosophy of the framework and how to use it such that by the time they complete this study, they will acquire knowledge of how to achieve a successful and sustainable project delivery.

Chapter 12

A Suggested Framework

The suggested framework consists of the following components as shown in Figure 12.1:

1. Vision
2. Mission
3. Goals, organisational strategy, strategic objectives and tactics
4. The Organisational Project Management (OPM)
5. PMOs in their three major forms of Enterprise or Strategic Project Management Office (EPMO), Project Portfolio Management Office (PPMO), Programme Management Office (PgMO) and Project Management Office (PMO)
6. High-level operations planning and management and Project Portfolio Planning and Management (PPM)
7. Management of ongoing operations including recurring activities producing benefits and values, and Management of Authorised Programme (PgM) and Projects (PM) including projected activities increasing value producing capability

Description of the Components of the Framework

1. Vision

As shown in the figure, the framework starts with a vision statement which states the desired future position of the organisation and be considered as a snapshot of its future. It is the main idea which drives the organisation

Figure 12.1 A suggested framework.

towards goals, benefits or other desired outcomes. It provides the basis and the foundation for the organisation's strategic planning. The vision will usually be a brief statement of intention communicated by the leadership.

Vision of an African company in project management could be as suggested in the following statement: It is the intention that in five years' time, their project management practice will be so structured that, when a project is being planned, its operation and sustainability will be considered. Estimates and forecasts of income to be earned, how, when and by whom they will be generated during the operation of the project deliverables will be built into the project plan. The estimates should include funds to be generated monthly by the commissioned and taken-over deliverable to finance the ongoing operation and maintenance of the deliverable, and to provide a planned return on investment (ROI). The objective is to ensure that it is profitable and competitive in the marketplace. These estimates should be included in the plan before the project plan is approved for implementation.

2. Mission

Next is the mission statement which presents the essence of the organisation. It states its business, goals and reason for existing.

The Mission Statement could be to achieve efficient delivery of sustainable project deliverables such that the planned benefits for which the projects are initiated and implemented will be harvested, utilised and sustained as planned. The deliverables will yield income and generate profits as planned.

3. Goals, Organisational Strategy, Strategic Objectives and Tactics

Goals could be defined as purposes or targets which a business aims to achieve.

Strategy: This is a statement of how it plans to go from its present to the future state. Organisations, regardless of their sizes or types exist to deliver value to their stakeholders. To achieve this, it will need a strategy as the expression of its vision and mission to deliver its intended value. The motivation of an organisation's strategy is the translation of its vision and mission into those actions that will deliver maximum value to its stakeholders, thus ensuring continual growth in business results. Whether it is a for-profit business, a not-for-profit service or a government agency, it will use a strategy to deliver its intended value.

A strategy statement should consist of the following components:

■ The objective or business goals
■ How it will be done; scope
■ Competitive advantage
■ Target audience

For example, the strategy statement could be to achieve success and sustainability in the delivery of projects by the use of the recommended framework such that the resulting deliverables should be used to accomplish socio-economic development and enhance competitiveness and high return on investment (ROI) in Africa.

It is essential to check that the adopted strategy contains and addresses the vision, objectives and mission accurately and aligns with them.

Strategic Objectives

Strategic objectives are statements of what the organisation intends to achieve. They have to be SMART; that is an acronym for Specific, Measurable, Achievable or Attainable, Realistic or Relevant and Time bound.

Objectives have to be created based on an organisation's strategy, not on its industry.

Balanced Scorecard and Strategic Objectives

The balanced scorecard (BSC) is a tool essential for strategy development and management. It is a strategic planning and management tool that is used extensively in business, industry, government and non-government and non-profit organisations to align business activities to the vision and strategy. It is used to improve internal and external communications and monitor organisational performance against strategic goals. The basis of the balanced scorecard is, "what gets measured, gets done" [1]. It helps organisations to establish how operational activities link to the strategy and provide measurable impact (Figure 12.2).

The following are the four basic viewpoints or perspectives of the balanced scorecard:

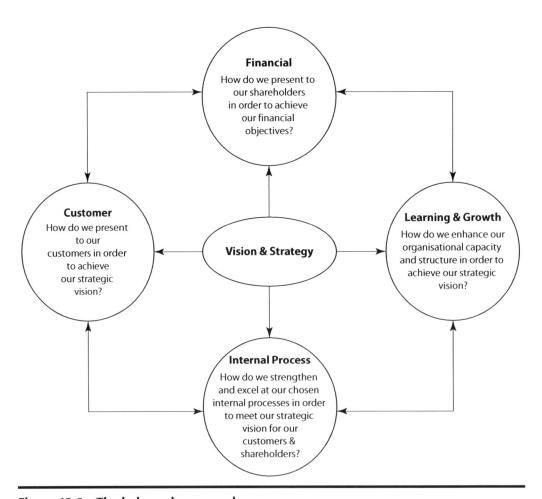

Figure 12.2 The balanced scorecard.

- **Financial perspective:** This tracks financial performance and views organisational financial performance and the use of financial resources.
- **Customer/stakeholder perspective:** This perspective views organisational performance from the point of view of the customer or other key stakeholders that the organisation is designed to serve, tracking customer satisfaction, attitudes and market share goals.
- **Internal process perspective:** This process views organisational performance through the lenses of the quality and efficiency related to our product or services or other key business processes. It covers internal operational goals needed to meet customer objectives and strategic goals.
- **The learning and growth or innovation perspective or organisational capacity:** It views organisational performance through human capital, infrastructure, technology, culture and other capacities that are key to breakthrough performance. It views intangible drivers for future success such as human capital, organisational capital, training, informational systems, etc.

The idea is that these four perspectives are interdependent and hierarchical as exemplified in the following paragraphs. Growth is driven by constant learning and innovation, which leads to the refinement of internal processes.

Examples and applications of the four perspectives which are financial, customer, internal processes and people (learning and growth) are as shown below:

Financial strategic objectives
    Financial growth: To exceed $10 million in the next 10 years.
    Financial efficiency: To increase net profit by 10% annually in the next five years.
Customer/constituent strategic objectives
    Current customers: To expand sales to existing customers.
    Current customers: To increase customer retention.
Internal/operational strategic objectives
    Product/service/programme management: To have all products meet standard of excellence guidelines.
    Operations management: To capitalise on physical facilities (location, capacity, etc.).
    Technology management: To increase efficiencies through use of wireless or virtual technology.

Channel management: To improve distributor and/or supplier relationships.

People/learning strategic objectives

People: To employ professionals who create success for customers.

Knowledge: To continually learn and adopt current best practices.

These are just examples of strategic objectives. The BSC connects the big picture strategy elements such as mission (our purpose), vision (what we aspire for), core values (what we believe in), strategic focus areas (themes, results and/or goals) and the more operational elements such as objectives (continuous improvement activities), measures (or key performance indicators, or KPIs, which track strategic performance), targets (our desired level of performance) and initiatives (projects that help achieve the targets).

■ All the four "perspectives" of the balanced scorecard should be considered when creating strategic objectives.

■ The format of each objective statement should be: Action (verb) + Description (adjective) + Result (noun).

■ The statement should state and clarify the objective. The objective statement should describe what the objective means and how it will be accomplished.

■ Objectives should link together as a group in a logical way. In other words, you shouldn't have one objective that states "Develop interpersonal relationships," and another that states, "Migrate everyone to an online support system." Be sure that all of your objectives work together in a way that reflects your strategy.

■ Every objective must have at least a verb and a noun: For example, a good objective statement is: improve fundraising. While a bad statement is: fundraising.

■ Remember that strategic objectives are long term and should be aligned with the organisation's mission and vision.

Planning and Implementation of Strategic Objectives

Merely having a strategy does not automatically ensure the delivery of the goals and benefits. It is only through the effective implementation of strategy will an organisation achieve its goals. Before the implementation, there should be a strategic planning process which should be undertaken by an organisation to develop a plan for the achievement of its overall goals [2].

It should include a situational analysis and an implementation plan.

Situational analysis: It consists of the following:

- Examining the current external and internal environment of the organisation.
- Formulating organisational objectives and strategies based upon the environmental assessment.
- Developing procedures to implement and evaluate the strategic plan.

A strategic plan may cover about a three-to-five-year period, but in a dynamic environment, it may be shorter.

Implementation Plan

This is necessary because it will turn the vision into reality and enhances efficiency and accountability for the following reasons:

- It describes how the organisation will achieve its objectives through detailed action steps.
- It discusses how the steps will be taken.
- It suggests when they will be taken.
- It identifies who will take them.

In effect, an implementation plan should consist of the following:

- Specify the actions to be carried out
- Name who will implement them
- Specify the times when they will take place, and their duration
- Specify the resources such as money, material and humans required
- List names of persons and officials who should be informed and kept in the communication loop

An implementation plan should be clear, current in that it is not discussing past events or actions that cannot be taken because the issues do no longer exist. It should be comprehensive, addressing every aspect of the objectives, mission and vision (Table 12.1).

Table 12.1 A Strategy Implementation Plan

Specific actions	Responsible persons	When to start	When to complete	Required resources (financial and material)	Obvious or imminent risks or problems	Persons to be kept informed

Other Important Factors for the Successful Implementation of Strategy

Effective and efficient implementation of an organisation's strategy requires other factors working in alignment for success. They include the following:

I. An accountability model for each element of the strategy must be clearly defined and embraced. It comprises:
   – Who is responsible for each of the organisation's strategic initiatives (these are projects, programmes and portfolios to be executed in order to implement strategy)?
   – Who is responsible for defining, collecting and reporting on the organisation's key performance indicators?
II. The strategy should be effectively cascaded down or translated into the business units, support functions, teams and individuals through the organisation.
III. Adequate resources (time, budget, skills and capacities) should be available. It is unhelpful to an organisation to invest time and money to develop a strategy, only to find that it does not have sufficient resources to implement it.
IV. Managing change on a consistent and professional basis is vital. Change management is the primary responsibility of the executive leadership team. It involves the understanding and managing of internal and external change and understanding the influencers of change.
V. Establishing a performance culture is a fundamental requirement for effective implementation.

   Strategies most often fail because they aren't executed well. Things that are supposed to happen don't happen. Either the organizations cannot make them happen, or the leaders of the business misjudge the challenges their companies face in the business environment, or both [3].

After creating the plan, review it for completeness. When it is implemented, monitor its performance. With this, performance management will be discussed next.

Performance Management

It is advisable to use key performance indicators in strategy performance management. Strategic key performance indicators monitor the implementation and effectiveness of an organisation's strategies, help to determine the gap between actual and targeted performance and determine organisation effectiveness and operational efficiency. KPIs use a metric for quantitatively assessing performance regarding the needs and expectations of stakeholders, the achievement of goals and reflecting the critical success factors.

A linkage is made between BSC and KPI to align operations management with organisational strategy. An essential function of key performance indicators and a balanced scorecard linkage is to align organisational performance with the strategic objectives of the company. When used in monitoring and measurements, the key performance indicators help determine if the performance of the organisation is moving in the right direction [4]. Notes on KPI, BSC and KPI-BSC linkage are given in Appendices 3, 7 and 8 respectively.

It is also a tool for monitoring the results of strategic decisions taken by the company from indicators already established. The resulting communication enables managers to reallocate physical, financial and human resources in order to achieve strategic objectives. In effect, a balanced scorecard is a tool for performance measurement used to identify and improve various functions of a business and their resulting external outcomes. It is used to measure and provide feedback to organisations. Note that while a balanced scorecard is used to measure performance at a point in time, it is different from a performance scorecard.

A performance Scorecard

A performance scorecard is a graphical representation of the progress over time of some entity, such as an enterprise, an employee or a business unit, towards some specified goals. Performance scorecards are widely used in many industries throughout the public and private sectors. The performance scorecard is an application of the balanced scorecard methodology.

Performance scorecards could be used independently of the balanced scorecard methodology to monitor the progress of any organisational goal. Performance scorecards are often said to be a visual answer to the question, "How are we doing?"

A structured measurement programme ensures that one can do the following:

■ Identify areas for performance improvement.
■ Benchmark against industry/competitors.
■ Set targets and measure performance.
■ Find the variance between current performance and benchmark.
■ Identify trends for forecasting and planning.
■ Evaluate the effectiveness of changes.

- Determine the impact on the organisation's performance.
- Amend or continue with the initiative to effect the change (Figure 12.3).

It is relevant to note the difference between benchmark and baseline. A baseline is an internally accepted reading or measurement with which subsequent readings can be compared. For example, in a project to improve

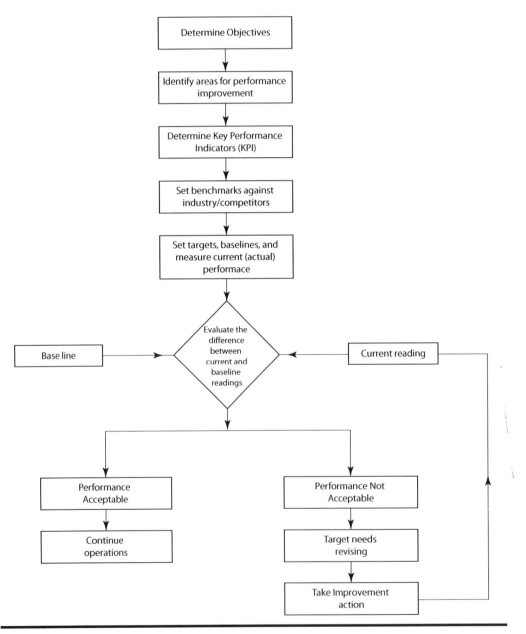

Figure 12.3 Procedure for performance measurement.

the income in a business; an income on 2 November is noted before the improvement activities are embarked upon. One month after, on 2 December, the income is checked again. The value recorded is compared with the value on 2 November, which is now the baseline. Incomes recorded in future months are still compared with the baseline which is the income recorded on 2 November. From the evaluated readings or differences between the monthly readings and the baseline, the improvement or otherwise, in the income caused by the improvement activities can be evaluated.

Unless an organisation is capturing, baselining, continuously monitoring and improving performance measurement practices, it will be unable to obtain an accurate picture of whether or not the organisation is actually realizing the value it has projected in its corporate strategic objectives and from its investments [5].

Project portfolio tracking is all about measurement. When accurate data is available, strategic decision makers can decide where to invest more, or less, effort. The data used must be accurate and current. When an organisation does not use a performance management programme, it will be difficult to determine whether the planned benefits of its projects and programmes are being realised. Performance measurement is therefore an essential component in benefits realisation management.

The necessity to establish benefits realisation programmes underscores the need for performance measurement. Organisations need to be able to measure and quantify the results from their investments in projects or in training; therefore, baseline performance measures have to be made, such that improvement can be monitored. It is not feasible to manage what you do not measure and you also cannot tell if it has improved or not.

As shown in Figure 12.3, targets and key performance indicators are essential in performance measurements. KPIs are metrics used to evaluate factors that are crucial to the success of an organisation; targets are specific goals for those indicators. There are many metrics for measurements. There is no single set of metrics that applies to all companies and industries. The appropriate set of metrics depends on the organisation's industry, strategy, technology and environment.

Success Story

This section contains a success story which was achieved by the use of key performance index and balanced scorecard in strategy management. The challenge is for us to learn to do the same (Table 12.2).

Table 12.2   Performance Scorecard

Strategic Objectives	Initiatives	Goals/targets	Metrics	Baseline	Current	Variance
Financial: To increase net profit	Enhance gross profit margin by expanding sales income and profits and reducing costs	By 10% annually in the next five years	Gross profit margin % = gross profit/net sales × 100	GPM on 15 Dec. 2018	GPM on 15 Dec. 2019	Difference
Customer: To increase sales	Expand productivity, especially among the sales team	To expand sales to all existing customers	Productivity = output/input	Productivity on 15 Dec. 2018	Productivity on 15 Dec. 2019	Difference
Internal: To enhance customer base	Increase sales to current customers and increase customer retention	To improve supplier/ distributor/ customer relationships	Sales revenue from customers	Sales on 15 Dec. 2018	Sales on 15 Dec. 2019	Difference
People: To enhance competency among staff	Provide relevant training and monitor performance	To employ professionals who create success for customers	Monitor post-course performance of staff on the job	Performance before the course	Performance six months after the course	Difference

Mecklenburg County Success Story of the Use of KPI and BSC in Strategy Management [6]

The Problem

Mecklenburg County is the largest county in North Carolina and the most urban. The County, which includes the city of Charlotte, has approximately 969,000 residents, and the population continues to grow at about 3% a year. In the late 1990s and early 2000s, the political majority of the board of county commissioners was changing after every two-year election cycle. The community and County staff suffered from rapidly changing priorities after every election.

Solution

In late spring 2001, the Board of County Commissioners for Mecklenburg County, North Carolina, had adopted a long-term vision for the community. It was summed up with the tagline: "In 2015, Mecklenburg County will be a community of pride and choice for people to LIVE, WORK and RECREATE."

County manager, Harry Jones, was charged with guiding the County to this vision. But Jones recognized that the County lacked a stable and sustainable approach to achieving the vision and it had no consistent model for making funding decisions based on priorities and assessing the bigger impact of those decisions. He decided the County needed to develop a model and structure for decision making that could be sustained regardless of economic conditions or political ideology. At the time, they had no way of predicting the long-term impact of this decision but the system he implemented led to breakthrough performance towards achieving the County's vision and the framework is, to this day, in use at Mecklenburg County.

The County manager and the board committed to the concept of the new framework, which was named Managing for Results (M4R). This framework would be centred on making data-driven decisions based on objective measurement of results achieved, using the balanced scorecard as the primary performance management tool. The main features of the framework are as follows:

- The board established the vision.
- It adopted the community and corporate scorecard.
- It carried out a strategic review of all county-funded programs.
- It conducted priority setting.
- It began making funding decisions based on all these factors.

While Managing for Results (M4R) has not removed political decision making completely, it has provided a more transparent process that allows more stability and sustainability in planning, budgeting and managing services in alignment with the County's vision [6].

Comments: The lesson of this case study is that it is rewarding to make data-driven decisions using KPIs and balanced scorecard.

4. Organisational Project Management (OPM): A Tool for Strategy Implementation

The fourth component in the framework is the Organisational Project Management (OPM). It is a strategy execution process utilising project, programme and portfolio management and organisational practices for consistent delivery of good performance, results and sustainable competitive advantages. It also uses the Enterprise Project Management Office (EPMO)

As already explained, the goal of an organisation's strategy is the translation of its vision and mission into those actions that will deliver maximum value to its stakeholders, thus ensuring continued growth in business results. Organisations are constantly seeking ways to improve their capabilities and performance in the delivery of strategy. Organisational Project Management (OPM) provides organisations with the means to this end. OPM is suggested for use in setting up the framework as it will deliver its strategy through a portfolio of programmes and projects that represent priority initiatives and changes deemed necessary for realising the delivery of organisational goals. Besides, an organisation in a commercial environment, whether in Africa or in developed nations, is not alone in its industry or market; it has competitors. It is therefore the case that in a competitive world, an organisation should manage its portfolios, programmes and projects efficiently to be able to succeed and maximise the values it delivers to its stakeholders.

PMI describes OPM as "a strategy execution framework utilizing project, programme, and portfolio management as well as organizational enabling practices to deliver consistently and predictably organizational strategy producing better performance, better results, and sustainable competitive advantage" [7].

OPM performs functions which include the following:

■ It aligns the development and implementation of strategy through the effective deployment of its portfolios of programmes and projects for the creation and delivery of strategic business results.

- It harmonises the strategic goals of the organisation with operations to ensure optimum assignment of talent, knowledge and capital resources.
- The key to effective fitting of the capabilities of OPM is a strategically positioned and implemented Enterprise Project Management Office (EPMO) – or a Strategic PMO – that can utilize all the described resources to ensure that functionality of OPM is offered to an organisation.

Some Strategic Functions of OPM

It is said that OPM provides an adaptive approach for fitting the capabilities of project, programme and portfolio management to the unique circumstances and needs of the organisation (Table 12.3).

How OPM Is Set Up and Used

OPM is crucial to achieving differentiated implementation and delivery of organisational strategy. It cuts across the organisation to provide a flexible, yet disciplined and systematic means of delivering strategy; hence, it is described as adaptive. It establishes a business focus for integrating and aligning the organisation to its purpose, providing a culture of engagement and continuous improvement.

By fitting the capabilities of project, programme and portfolio management to the unique circumstances and needs of the organisation, the PMO can achieve the goals of OPM which are better performance, better results and sustainable competitive advantage through continuous improvement in the delivery of its strategy.

For portfolio managers, OPM provides a framework to align the work and resources of the organisation to strategy while giving programme managers greater visibility of the short- and long-term strategic goals. Furthermore, emphasis is on the essential nature of a strategically positioned PMO in ensuring the effective implementation of OPM and maturing of capabilities

Table 12.3 Some Strategic Functions of OPM

Actions Required	Components	Execution
Develop strategy	Vision, organisational strategy and objectives	Develop
Implement OPM	High-level operations management and portfolio management	Deploy
	Ongoing operations management, and programme and project management	Deliver

that will deliver the organisation's goals of better performance, better results and a sustainable competitive advantage.

Implementation of OPM

OPM is an ongoing programme for as long as an organisation performs projects, programmes and portfolios. For the implementation of OPM, it is considered necessary to make the following points:

1. Gap analysis and initiatives

- The implementation should be started with a gap analysis which shows the difference or gap between the current state of the organisation's strategy and project management practices and desired future state of the organisation.
- Gap analysis could be performed by comparing current organisational performance with the desired performance using KPIs.
- With the gap analysis defined, the next phase is the identification and alignment of initiatives and the development of an implementation roadmap for OPM.
- The gap analysis data is used to identify the list of initiatives (i.e. portfolio, programmes and projects) that can be used to address the gap.
- These initiatives should be identified with the corporate objectives and metrics. The metrics will provide the information that will help in the selection and prioritisation of the initiatives in line with the corporate strategy.
- The initiatives are reviewed by a team of stakeholders and prioritised based on the organisational needs, fit, desired future state, resource-sharing issues with other initiatives and projects in the organisation, business timelines and strategy alignment.
- These initiatives are grouped into portfolios to be executed at predetermined periods. Portfolios and therefore programmes derived from them are aligned to organisational strategy.
- In effect, portfolio management aligns with organisational strategies by selecting the right programmes, project and operational work; prioritising the work; and providing the necessary resources. Programme management harmonises programmes and projects and controls interdependence to realise identified benefits in accordance with organisational strategic objectives. Project management develops and implements plans to achieve a specific scope as

driven by the objectives of the programme, portfolio and organisational strategy.

1. Implementation of initiatives

The next step in the implementation phase is to prepare the implementation plan for each initiative. While the implementation roadmap provides a long-term plan for the implementation of the OPM, the implementation plan gives the details required to implement the roadmap. It is recommended that the following steps could be used to implement the OPM:

Determine requirements for each initiative: The following factors could be considered when developing requirements.

■ Characteristics of projects such as size, risk, work contents, etc.
■ Budgets
■ Resource availability
■ Submitted requests for change
■ Lessons learned, etc.

Develop tailored components of initiatives: This could mean the decision to buy or build, its ability to support different initiatives and available resources.

■ The implementation should be based on good programme management practice and the subordinate plans that constitute a programme management plan.
■ It should include a schedule that contains deliverables, due dates, responsibilities, steering committee meetings, etc.
■ Develop the following components of programme management which are specific to implementing OPM:
■ **Benefits realisation plan:** It shows how and when the selected benefits will be delivered to the organisation.
■ **Resource management plan:** This involves developing a plan for identifying, securing and managing OPM core resources.
■ **Organisational change management plan:** With a clear understanding of current state of the organisations, initiate and manage change for initiatives that modify their environment, processes and tools to enable them to work towards attaining the desired state. This also involves effective leadership and management of human factors.

- **Risk management plan:** This entails effective management of risks to the OPM implementation plan and secondary risks generated by the OPM to the organisation.
- **Key performance indicators:** Define KPIs for performance tracking and monitoring. These will become the metrics for measuring delivery of expected benefits. It is therefore necessary to capture a baseline prior to OPM implementation in order to determine how much the OPM implementation has changed the values of the KPIs.
- **Use of pilot:** If a pilot is used, the detailed implementation plan could be amended from the results obtained after the pilot has been concluded based on the lessons learned. After the amendment, a new OPM policy should be issued and distributed to all stakeholders, team members, etc.
- **Realise benefits:** In order to measure benefits derived from OPM implementation, it is necessary that for each KPI metric, a baseline value should be measured and recorded before the implementation of OPM is started. With this, it should be possible to determine the improvement achieved by the OPM implementation by measuring the value of the KPI metric when the improvement is required.
- **Continuous improvement:** It is advisable that the OPM implementation should be based on a continuous improvement policy. The discovery and analysis should be conducted periodically, probably annually, to discover the state of the OPM and which aspects should require improvements. It is also advisable to change members of the OPM implementation team from time to time to ensure that members of the team are still informed on the operations and activities of the organisation.

OPM Monitoring, Strategy Deployment and Review, Performance Monitoring

An organisation's portfolio of programmes and projects represents those investments that management believes to be most significant and necessary to succeed in its chosen market(s). It does not matter how well an organisation manages its programmes or executes its projects; if they are the wrong initiatives, the entire effort will amount to a lost opportunity. Not only is the deployment of strategy into a balanced portfolio crucial, it is also an essential step in the allocation of scarce organisational resources to ensure maintenance of efficient and effective operations.

Strategy development with deployment of the portfolio is not a one-off activity. Although a portfolio is typically deployed to represent a specific planning period, it must be reviewed periodically in the context of a rapidly changing global environment to ensure its continued relevance and ability to deliver intended business results. Accordingly, the mix of initiatives represented in the portfolio may undergo change during both the short- and long-term horizons. This underscores the need for continual monitoring of the performance of the portfolios of programmes and projects in order to ensure continuous improvement.

5. PMOs in Their Three Major Forms of Enterprise or Strategic Project Management Office (EPMO), Programme Management Office (PgMO) and Project Management Office (PMO)

In order to optimise the capabilities of OPM, a Strategic or Enterprise Project Management Office (PMO) is necessary. It helps in the achievement of the organisational strategy by utilising the organisation's resources to bridge the gap that exists between the current and future strategic positions of the organisation. In effect, it aligns the portfolio of programmes and projects to the business strategy.

PMOs: Project Management Offices

The definition of the PMO outlined by the Project Management Institute (PMI) (2004) is as follows [7]:

> An organizational body or entity assigned various responsibilities related to the centralized and coordinated management of those projects under its domain. The responsibilities of the PMO can extend from providing project management support functions to actually being responsible for the direct management of a project.

A PMO should be the unit responsible for building the OPM System and managing it. Different PMOs are used by project offices to support project/ programme/portfolio administrations as follows:

■ Project Management Offices (PMOs) to support obtaining successful projects.
■ Programme Management Offices to support getting and sustaining the benefits from projects/programmes.

■ Project Portfolio Management Offices to support achieving the strategic business goals.

It may be necessary to elaborate on the various forms of PMOs which could be used in the framework as a tool for resolving the problems of failure and abandonment of projects. There are three basic models of PMOs shown in Figure 12.4.

Strategic PMO: At the strategic level, the problem is one of resource limitation and achieving the strategic objective; the PMO plays the role of "Portfolio" Management Office as described in the next section (Figure 12.4).

Business PMO: At the Programme Control Level, a "Programme" Management Office does the following:
– It takes a multi-project perspective, reallocating project resources as needed when the programme manager focuses on a benefit.
– At this level, a programme management is implemented to the point that project selection and prioritisation can be done.

Project Control PMO: At the Project Control Level, a "Project" Management Office provides a project centre of excellence to oversee execution and control of projects. At this basic level, a project implementation plan is presented; the PMO is involved in project development and management functions.

The Role of a Strategic or Enterprise PMO (EPMO)
Enterprise Project Management Office does the following functions:

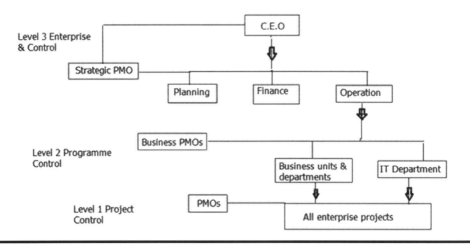

Figure 12.4 Levels of PMOs in an enterprise.

- It advises on investment opportunities and the achieving of the strategic objectives.
- It provides tools and techniques to the portfolio team for project prioritisation, midstream evaluation and strategic alignment.
- At this level, a PPM is implemented and developed such that it can select and prioritise programmes.

The Strategic PMO should have the authority to do the following:

- Align the portfolio of programmes and projects to business strategy
- Customize programme and project management practices
- Enhance governance and accountability
- Optimize the investment of the portfolio of programmes and projects
- Manage talent
- Ensure stakeholder buy-in
- Drive needed change
- Proactively navigate risk

These functions of the EPMO are expounded in subsequent paragraphs and in detail in Appendix 4. By fitting the capabilities of project, programme and portfolio management to the unique circumstances and needs of the organisation, the PMO can ensure the goals of better performance, better results and sustainable competitive advantage through continuous improvement in the delivery of its strategy. The Strategic PMO can utilize all the described resources to bridge the gap that exists between having knowledge of OPM and realisation of the potential it offers an organisation.

Most notably, PricewaterhouseCoopers (PwC) published a third global survey (2012) of more than 1,500 participants, from more than 30 industries and almost 40 countries, called *Insights and Trends: Current Portfolio, Programme, and Project Management Processes* (2012) [8]. In addition, PMI released its annual *Pulse of the Profession 2011* (2012), *Driving Success in Challenging Times* [9], an annual survey of more than 1,000 project, programme and portfolio managers around the world. Both surveys validate what has long been reported, that is, Strategic PMOs can be the vehicle organisations count on to move from business as usual, to making programme and project management a central component of their strategy.

6. "High-Level Operations Planning and Management" and "Project Portfolio Planning and Management"

These are the initiatives required to achieve the organisation's goals and are considered in Project Portfolio Management (PPM). In PPM, they are analysed for the efficient management of resources to produce the desired results. Therefore, the selection and prioritisation of programmes and projects are conducted in the analysis.

Before embarking on a programme, an organisation should conduct feasibility studies to clarify and define programme objectives, requirements, risks and to ensure alignment with organisation's strategic objectives.

As stated in the earlier paragraphs, the strategic plans are subdivided into organisational initiatives as determined by market dynamics, customer and partner requests, shareholders, government regulations, competitors' plans and actions. These initiatives are grouped into portfolios to be executed at predetermined periods. Portfolios, and therefore programmes and projects derived from them, are aligned to organisational strategy. Strategic planning and portfolio management processes which identify and measure benefits for the organisation identify the programmes that will produce the benefits as their expected outcome and results. In effect, organisations embark on programmes to deliver identified benefits which will accomplish agreed outcomes in line with the organisation's strategic objectives. From this, its objectives are developed. They are practical statements of its goals and will constitute the achievement of the strategy.

7. Management of Ongoing Operations Including Recurring Activities Producing Benefits and Values and "Management of Authorized Programs and Projects"

These appear at the bottom of the framework, correspond to executing the operations, programmes and project activities to realise the organization's strategic goals.

The "Project Portfolio Planning and Management" represents the relationship between the organisational strategy, strategic planning and management activities. To guide "the Management of Authorized Programs and Projects," a strategic project portfolio is created. This project portfolio links the organisational strategy to a set of prioritised programmes and projects and addresses the relevant internal and external business drivers referenced as objectives in the strategic plan.

Project Portfolio Management, Programme Management and Project Management including a discussion of benefits management are covered in the subsequent chapters.

Questions

i. What is an organisation's strategy? Why is it important?

ii. What are strategic objectives? What characteristic features should objectives have?

iii. Discuss how you can develop and implement strategic objectives.

iv. What is an organisational performance measurement? Why is it important?

v. The OPM contains the EPMO, PgMO and PMO. What do these acronyms stand for in project management?

vi. Distinguish between EPMO, PgMO, and PMO? Why are these important?

References

1. Axisto Consulting, "The business balanced scorecard and key performance indicators, the principles and approach to build," Axisto B.V. Amsterdam, The Netherlands, Fall 2019.

2. Jenette Nagy and Stephen B. Fawcett, "Strategic planning or 'VMOSA' (vision, mission, objectives, strategies, and action plans)," VMOSA – Strategic Planning techniques and technology for life. www.vmosa.net

3. Larry Bossidy and Ram Charan, "Execution: the discipline of getting things done by," Altfield Inc, Strategic Planning Marketing and Sales Consultants. 2002.

4. "Measuring performance, KPIs and the link to strategic objectives," www.pwc.co.uk/corporate reporting

5. L. Bull, K. Shaw and C. Baca, "Delivering strategy: organizational project management and the strategic PMO." Paper presented at PMI® Global Congress 2012—North America, Vancouver, British Columbia, Canada. Newtown Square, PA: Project Management Institute, 2012.

6. "Mecklenburg county success story of the use of KPI and BSC in strategy management," http://balancedscorecard.vn/hoc-lieu/hoc-lieu-tu-bsc/examples-and-success-stories.aspx

7. PM BokGuide, A Guide to the Project Management Body of Knowledge, 3rd edition, Project Management Institute (PMI) (2004), p.17.

8. *Insights and Trends: Current Portfolio, Programme, and Project Management Processes* (2012) Insights and Trends: Current Portfolio, Programme, and Project Management Practices The third global survey on the current state of project management 2012 Pricewaterhouse Coopers.

9. PMI's Pulse of the Profession, Driving Success in Challenging Times, 2012 series.

Chapter 13

Project Portfolio Management (PPM)

An Introduction to Project Portfolio Management

PPM is the management of portfolios, programmes, projects and operations as initiatives for converting corporate strategic objectives into products and services to achieve the goals of the organisations. It uses strategic planning to establish the portfolios required to achieve corporate strategic objectives and goals. It is relevant to note that a portfolio is a collection of projects and programmes managed in a coordinated way to obtain benefits and control not available from managing them individually and other works that are grouped together to facilitate effective management to meet strategic business objectives. The following explanations are also relevant:

- Portfolio management is the organisation of multiple projects into a single portfolio that allows for the balanced management of the projects. Strong portfolio management clarifies projects as investments; prevents the loss of value by guiding on-time, on-cost, quality delivery of projects; and substantiates benefit realisation.
- Enterprise-wide project performance gates could be used to ensure that standard performance metrics are met before a project is permitted to continue. Similar metrics are used in maturing approval processes for every identified work order.
- Portfolio management must be designed to report weighted performance of selected projects and work orders against these metrics.

■ Portfolio management achieves strategic goals by selecting, prioritising, assessing, and managing projects, programmes and other related works based upon their alignment and contribution to the organisation's strategies and objectives.

Functions and Necessity

The impact of portfolio on corporate strategic objectives is achieved through six activities as discussed in the next paragraphs:

■ **Maintaining portfolio strategic alignment:** Each portfolio component is aligned to an aspect of the strategic objective which it should achieve when it is implemented.
■ **Allocating financial resources:** The priority of each portfolio component determines its financial allocation for its execution.
■ **Allocating human resources:** Priority of a component determines its human resources allocation for its execution.
■ **Allocating material and equipment resources:** This is also determined by its priority and its long-term investment.
■ **Measuring component performance:** The performance of each portfolio component is measured to determine how well it contributes to the achievement of the corporate strategic objective, and this is necessary for its continual existence.
■ **Managing risks:** Each component should be evaluated for risks to determine how this affects its performance and contribution towards achieving the corporate strategic goals.

Functions: Project portfolio management has at least seven major functions [1]:

■ Determining a viable project mix, one that is capable of meeting the goals of the organisation.
■ Balancing the portfolio, to ensure a mix of projects that balances short term versus long term, risk versus reward, research versus development, operation versus project, etc.
■ Monitoring the planning and execution of the chosen projects
■ Analysing portfolio performance and ways to improve it
■ Evaluating new opportunities against the current portfolio and considering the organisation's project execution capacity

- Providing information and recommendations to decision makers at all levels
- Bridging the gap between strategic planning and implementation

A more holistic understanding of project portfolio management

It is suggested that a more complete picture of PPM is provided by a Project Portfolio Life Span (PPLS) that consists of the following five phased components:

- Identification of needs and opportunities (corporate fiscal planning)
- Selection of best combinations of projects (project portfolio management)
- Planning and execution of projects (project management)
- Product launch and deployment of project deliverables (marketing and sales)
- Realisation of benefits (operation, corporate due diligence and accounting)

It is necessary that the data generated by the last two phases should be collected and fed back to the project portfolio management process. This feedback enables the validation of the assumptions of project portfolio management and provides information on the benefits produced. It is essential that to measure the success attained in project portfolio management, it has to be ascertained that the extent to which the intended benefits from project portfolio management function has been obtained. To achieve this, there should be a process or system for tracking and analysing the feedback of the benefits achieved. It is essential that data so collected be linked to specific projects [2].

The PPM Philosophy

PPM is the management of the programmes and projects to maximise their contributions to the overall success of the enterprise. It bridges the gap between the programmes, projects and the operations of the business. It enables us not only to do programmes and projects right but also to select and do the right programmes and projects [3]. Its philosophy can be described as follows:

- As a process, it starts with a prioritisation and selection procedure of programmes and projects.

- It evaluates a proposed programme against a set of selection criteria such that bad programmes are eliminated or modified to be acceptable. In effect, PPM is about having the right information so that the right decisions can be made to select the right programmes and projects.
- It evaluates values and benefits, by modifying benefit calculations on the basis of risk.
- It ensures that analyses are made under structured and consistent procedures such that programmes and projects that will cause problems are eliminated from the portfolios.
- It evaluates benefits, risks, alignment and other business matters such that programmes and projects can be ranked, prioritised and selected for implementation.
- It monitors the performance of active projects against both the project goals and the selection criteria so that the portfolio can be selected to maximise return. This means being willing to restructure, delay or even terminate projects with performance deficiencies.
- It does not preclude preparing traditional business plans and analyses because PPM helps in dealing with multiple business plans and opportunities.
- Portfolio planning is based extensively on forecasting. Levine, the author, whose work is modified and adapted in this book, writes that "forecasting is like driving an automobile while blindfolded and taking directions from someone who is looking out of the back window" [3]. It is therefore necessary to be careful in staking the future of the company on such data. However, with recent developments in Business Intelligence and Web Analytics, forecasting can now be made with more confidence. This does not mean that all that will happen in the future of the business can be confidently predicted.

Implementation of Project Portfolio Management

For implementation purposes, PPM can be subdivided into two primary phases. The first is prioritising and selecting projects for the portfolio, and the second is processing and managing the projects within the portfolio. These two phases require different practices and affect each other; they must be integrated. However, before working on these phases, there are

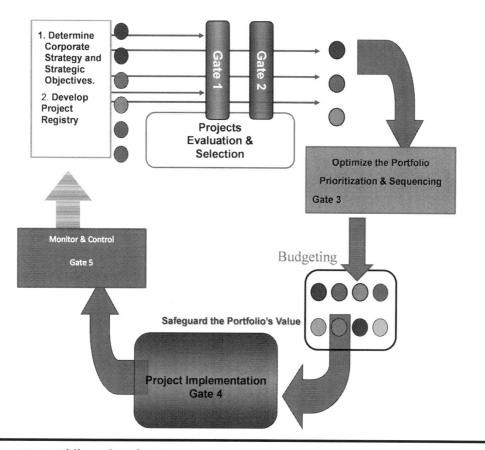

Figure 13.1   Philosophy of PPM process.

some corporate planning operations that need to be done. These have been discussed earlier and include the following (Figure 13.1):

- Develop the corporate strategic plan
- Decide and define on the benefits and values derivable from each aspect of the plan
- Decide on the number of projects and programmes that are required to implement and achieve the benefits
- Determine the budgets and the organisation's resources that can be invested in the portfolio
- Establish a set of weighted scoring criteria for the prioritisation of projects
- Establish guidelines for determining acceptable risks

Describing and Developing the Phases

Gate or Phase 1: Classification, Evaluation and Selection

After a decision that an initiative could be treated as a project, all the projects so initiated are classified. Projects of the portfolio are prioritised on the basis of their strategic significance, financial benefit, project types, project complexity, risk level, and resource needs (finance, human, material, equipment). This process can be described as follows:

- Making project proposals (business case) so that each project can be evaluated
- Evaluating project value and benefits
- Identifying the risks that might modify these benefits
- Making sure that each of these benefits from the projects facilitates the achievement of corporate strategies
- Determining the most favourable use of resources in the projects
- Ranking the projects according to an established set of selection criteria
- Selecting the projects for the portfolio

Necessity for Evaluation and Selection

- Sadly, much effort is invested in doing projects right or correctly which may not be the right projects. Why?
- Some approved projects may not deliver the expected benefits.
- Some are wrong projects because they are incompatible with corporate strategy.
- Some approved projects have unacceptable risks.
- Some projects are approved because of the political power of their sponsors.
- Some projects start failing right from the onset, yet they are continued until their complete failure becomes obvious.

These projects remove scarce resources from more beneficial projects. They are a liability and not an asset to the company. The PPM process helps to eliminate them and minimise the occurrence of failed projects. It tries to ensure that they are not embarked upon in the first place so that no resources are wasted on them.

Gate or Phase 2: Management and Monitoring

This phase consists of processing and managing the projects within the portfolio. The projects are managed with a view to achieve the following:

- To meet the project's objectives, that is produce the agreed deliverable while completing the project on time, on budget, in quality and scope. These could be achieved with the traditional project management tracking and control processes.
- To ensure that the project is used to obtain the benefits and values assigned to it from the corporate strategic plan to achieve the corporate strategic objectives.

The process can be described as follows:

- As the project is being implemented, it is necessary to monitor and evaluate any conditions that may change the project's characteristics or selection criteria.
- Periodically, it is necessary to update or confirm the continuing validity of criteria used for project selection.
- On an agreed regular basis, the status and performance of each project needs to be monitored. If the performance falls so low that it cannot produce the benefits and values assigned to the project at the proposal stage, it may be necessary to determine whether the project should remain or be removed from the portfolio.
- Terminating an active project may not always be possible or wise. However, all options, including its contributions to other projects in its programmes and the entire portfolio, should be considered.
- Earned value analysis and the Stage Gate process could be used in the periodic evaluation of project status and performance.

Gate or Phase 3: Business Plan and Budgeting

Business plans and budgeting are inputs to the PPM process because they may have to deal with multiple business plans and opportunities.

Gate or Phase 4: Project Implementation

As has been discussed earlier in this section, PPM can be subdivided into two primary phases. The first has already discussed; the second phase is briefly touched on the next.

For the second phase, monitoring and control of projects, programmes and portfolios as well as project registry are considered.

Monitoring and Control

Flexibility, Continuity and Key Performance Index

Portfolio implementation is a continuous process such that in the changing business environments, portfolios have a business scope that changes with strategic goals of the organisations. Portfolio management is an ongoing process with the purpose of maximising the return on the investment of the portfolio and projects in order to meet the organisation's strategic objectives. It is essential to determine how each objective is met. For this purpose, the Key Performance Index (KPI) is required. As discussed earlier in this book, a KPI is a numerical or quantitative indicator that can be used to determine how well each objective is being met.

Other Applications of KPIs in PPM

They are tools that enhance the understanding of the performance of each project when it is interconnected with the performance of other projects and linked with strategic objectives. Their functions include the following:

- They help measure the achievement of a portfolio's strategic objectives taking into account the realisation of key benefits. This approach helps identify strategic interdependences between the constituent projects of the portfolio.
- This interdependence facilitates the understanding of how the performance of a single project affects the overall performance of the portfolio of projects. This is one of the reasons why care has to be taken over a decision to terminate any project.
- As a result of these functions, the strategic performance of several projects can be tracked. It should then be feasible to determine the achievement of the corporate strategic objectives. This may not be possible if individual projects are considered in isolation.

Even as the applications of KPIs in project portfolio management are being considered, it is essential that Critical Success Factors (CSF) of PPM are considered. These are the necessary factors that have to be met for success. One of these is the need to adapt corporate strategy to changing environmental business and economic conditions, both internally and externally. Strategy implementation should be adapted to changing external and internal events that affect the company's operations.

Using BSC to Implement Corporate Strategy Using PPM

In practice, such tools as the balanced scorecard (BSC) and metrics linked with KPIs are used for implementing corporate strategy with PPM. As discussed earlier, BSC includes four perspectives for translating a strategy into action, which are financial, customer, internal learning and growth. A strategy map for a balanced scorecard describes the strategic process for transforming intangible assets into tangible customer and financial outcomes. The balanced scorecard transforms an organisation's strategic plan from an attractive but passive document into the "marching orders" of activities for the organisation on a daily basis. It provides a framework that not only presents performance measurements, but helps planners identify what should be done and measured. It enables executives to truly execute their strategies.

For clarity purposes, a strategy map contains about 15 to 25 linked strategic objectives. Each objective will contain associated projects and processes. It will also contain appropriate KPI measures and targets, and key risk indicators.

PPM Governance

The "governance of project, programme and portfolio management is not a separate entity from that of the organisation because governance is an integrated and holistic process and is the exclusive responsibility of the governing body, typically a board of directors. It is impossible to govern one aspect of the business without affecting other aspects. Therefore, the governance of the management of Projects, Programs and Portfolios (PPP) (sometimes called "project governance" for convenience) is a sub-set of corporate and organisational governance, focused on assisting and ensuring that the projects and programmes undertaken by the organisation deliver the maximum value to the organisation. As a fundamental principle, we do not "govern project management" – we govern the organisation that undertakes projects as a part of its business. It is also important to differentiate the governance function from the techniques used to implement governance such as portfolio management and the management of project management.

These explanations are relevant:

1. The governance of the management of PPP, hereafter represented as PPM governance, fits within the overall governance of the organisation and is therefore the ultimate responsibility of the board of directors. PPM governance encompasses both project, programme and portfolio management governance and the governance of supporting management systems such as PMOs and project control boards (PCBs).

2. It focuses on overseeing the management systems that ensure that the right projects and programmes are selected by the organisation to achieve its strategic objectives, and that those selected are accomplished as efficiently as possible within the policy framework.

   In some "projectized organisations," the projects undertaken for clients represent the primary value stream for the organisation (its "sales"), and in every organisation, projects and programmes are a key element in the overall change process needed to adapt and grow the organisation to achieve its strategic objectives. The objectives of programmes and projects have to be aligned to the strategic objectives as explained in the following paragraphs:

3. Within the PPM system, it is essential that there is a clear determination of the projects' roles and responsibilities. Two key facets are accountability and the delegating of responsibility as discussed below:

   – The accountable person is the individual who is ultimately answerable for the outcomes of the project or programme and holds the ultimate authority and veto power. Only one accountable person should be assigned. There should be a statement that defines to whom the accountable person is accountable (e.g. a project sponsor is accountable to the board).

   – A responsible person is an individual who is responsible for completing the task. The responsible person manages the project or programme implementation. Responsibility can be explicitly shared between individuals. The degree of responsibility should be determined by the individual with the "accountability." As an example, a project sponsor is accountable (to the board) for the success (benefits realisation) of a project. And that sponsor can delegate responsibility to a project manager to deliver the project. The project manager can further delegate responsibility for the delivery of an element of the project deliverables to a supplier project manager via contract. But the sponsor is still accountable for project success. Both of these roles are important (and not having a clearly accountable executive, supported by responsible managers, is a recipe for failure).

4. The role of governance, that is the role of the board and executive management, is to ensure that the organisation is structured and operates such that capable and willing people are assigned to these key positions. And, additionally, they understand what aspects of governance responsibility and authority have been delegated to them along with their management responsibilities to execute the job done properly. The following are a number of key roles that support the governance system in ensuring successful project outcomes:

   – The sponsor is the key management link between the executive/strategic levels of the organisation and the managers responsible for the effective delivery of a project or programme.

   – Depending on the structure of the organisation, it is also quite likely that other senior managers will have some responsibilities to assist in the effective governance of the project or programme; the sponsor is responsible for leading and coordinating these inputs.

   – The PMO will have key roles in the areas of good practice, assurance and reporting to ensure accurate information is passed up to the board. A key role of the governing body is ensuring these systems are designed, effective and working properly.

Tips for Achieving Good Governance

■ The art of good governance is balancing rules and objectives to empower people to be successful and deliver good governance. It is having enough processes in place to prevent malfeasance – that is dishonest and illegal behaviour, whilst encouraging effective growth and innovation to achieve the strategic objectives of the organisation.

■ The foundation for this type of governance is creating a culture focused on doing the right things, the right way.

■ The design of the governance system is also a key consideration, creating a network of people with distributed power, decision making and information flows. It creates a variety of independent channels of communication and oversight, which facilitate localised decision making, internal contestability and cross checking, which, in a well-designed system, increase the reliability of the information flowing back up the organisation for management and governance purposes.

■ Culture is still the key – in this type of distributed environment, everyone needs to be focused on the good of the organisation and achieving good governance, not "petty politics. Processes, procedures and rules are important and useful as long as they assist in the overall objectives defined above.

■ In effect, PPM governance provides processes that ensure the effective and efficient use of resources in enabling an organisation to achieve its goals. It ensures that an organisation aligns PPM processes with business strategy, such that companies stay on track to achieve their strategies and goals. Governance guides the implementation of appropriate approaches to measure project performance. It ensures that all stakeholders' interests are considered and that processes provide measurable results.

Design of PPM Governance System

A PPM governance framework should answer some key questions, such as how the projects are functioning overall, what key metrics management needs and what is the return on investment. A good governance structure is central to making PPM work. "Portfolio management without governance is an empty concept" [3]. The key elements in PPM governance include:

■ Specifying the distribution of rights and responsibilities among different participants in the organisation.
■ Defining the rules and procedures for making decisions.
■ Defining the strategic framework needed to select the "right" projects and programmes to undertake.
■ Encouraging the efficient use of resources.
■ Monitoring performance.
■ Ensuring proper support for the organisational change needed to realise the intended benefits.
■ Requiring accountability at all levels for the stewardship of the organisation.
■ The art of good governance is designing systems that offer sufficient checks and balances to ensure accountability without diminishing the ability of the project and programme managers to deliver the objectives they have been tasked to accomplish. Governance structures and

processes are merely the mechanisms needed to achieve good governance; they do not represent good governance in themselves.

▪ As already stated, an essential factor for developing an effective governance framework that makes efficient use of these processes is cultural. Well-governed organisations develop an open culture focused on achieving excellence through the creation of meaningful ownership structures in which senior managers take responsibility for the work and its outcomes (of which governance is the enabler), supported by a proactive stakeholder focus which aligns the interests of key stakeholders – governance, authority and responsibility.

Other Features of PPM Governance System

▪ PPM governance ensures that the management develops and implements systems such that the right projects and programmes are selected by the organisation, and that the selected initiatives are accomplished as efficiently as possible.

▪ It involves setting the "right objectives," and then asking the "right questions" so that the governing board can be confident that the organisation's management is making the best use of the resources assigned to undertake projects and programmes. The "questions" asked by the board need firstly to assure that the management structures providing the answers to its questions is capable, effective and honest and then assure that the resources as deployed by the management are generating the optimum value to support the long-, medium- and short-term objectives defined in the organisation's strategy. The management's role is to understand the board's strategy and objectives and develop systems that are capable of offering effective "answers" to both sets of questions as well as providing advice and recommendations for improvements.

▪ Portfolio management should be focused on selecting the right projects and programmes to undertake in support of the strategy and terminating the ones that no longer contribute value to the organisation.

▪ Project sponsorship provides the direct link between the executive and the project or programme manager and is focused on the whole project life cycle, leading to the delivery of value.

▪ PMOs should be established to provide oversight and strategic reporting capabilities.

▪ The effective management of projects and programmes is the measure of an effective governance system.

PPM Governance and Portfolio Management

Portfolio management is a key management function to support the organisation's governance process by ensuring the selected projects are aligned with and support the organisation's strategy. It focuses on selecting the right projects and programmes to maintain, start, defer or delete. These decisions are based on what should be the best mix to achieve the organisations longer-term strategies, whilst maintaining current operations.

Governance Implications within the PMO

- PMOs have a critical governance support role; they need to ensure that accurate information is available to the executive management on the performance and trends of the projects and programmes.
- PMO management needs to ensure sufficient discipline and rigour in its processes to achieve the reporting accuracy needed, whilst allowing development and innovation to achieve the strategic objectives of the organisation.
- The two key functions of the PMO perform are, firstly, to ensure that information in its reports is useful, relevant, accurate and comprehensive and then, secondly, to provide interpretive and predictive assessments to help senior management fulfil its governance responsibilities and to support the portfolio management decision-making process.

Governance at the Programme and Project Level

- Projects and programmes are created by the organisation to deliver the change needed to achieve its objectives. The obligation of project and programme managers is to deliver the outputs and deliverables as efficiently as possible, whilst working ethically within the organisation's practices and procedures. If the governance system is working effectively, the organisation's projects and programmes will be managed effectively.
  1. The British Standard for project management, BS6079-1:200 Project management: Provides principles and guidelines for the management of projects. It defines four layers of governance and management:

- Governance related to identifying projects, approving them and assessing outcomes
- Governance of sponsorship through the project sponsor or delegate directing the project
- Governance of the management through the project manager initiating, managing and closing the project
- Governance of delivery through team managers, supported by their teams, creating the project's outputs

  The organisation's management should ensure that the appropriate project organisation is in place to undertake the project. All projects should have people identified and responsible for:
- Ensuring that managerial and technical oversight is maintained.
- Sponsoring projects in pursuit of stated organisational objectives. The sponsor's responsibility includes the completion of the project for organisational change, the application of the project's deliverables into operations and the realisation of the benefits.
- Managing the project on a day-to-day basis, ensuring that the deliverables are appropriate to the delivery of the desired outcomes. The project manager is accountable to the project sponsor for the day-to-day leadership and management of the project, the project team and all necessary functions.
- Undertaking the specialist work on the project, depending on the specific project. These roles may be supplemented by project support staff who are specialists in disciplines such as legal, finance, planning, risk management and procurement.

Decision makers should always be accountable to higher level management for key decisions relating to the project. They may be individuals or groups of people (e.g. boards) with the appropriate level of authority, skills and knowledge. The levels of authority and constituency of any decision-making body will normally be defined within the governance arrangements or schemes of delegation of the sponsoring organisation. For projects, external management approval and oversight is typically required for:

- Authorising the start of projects and each phase of a project
- Authorising changes to the project
- Changing the status of a project
- Ensuring compliance with the organisation's policies
- Ensuring compliance with any applicable legal or regulatory requirements

Reference: PPP Governance [4]. This White Paper is part of Mosaic's Project Knowledge Index to view and download a wide range of published papers and articles.

Tips for success in PPM are given in Appendix 5.

Management of Corporate Benefits in PPM Implementation, Challenges and Maintenance of PPM Implementation: Suggested Checklist of Key Components Required for Successful Project Portfolio Management

A portfolio brings together all benefits delivered by programmes and projects. It has a critical function to ensure that all benefits are aligned to the portfolio's strategic objectives. The role of a portfolio of projects is to ensure that the expected benefits are planned, realistic and in fact delivered by programmes and projects to facilitate the achievement of corporate strategy.

Benefit management: Why is benefit management necessary? Projects are undertaken to deliver benefits, but often they fail to achieve them. Research findings show that over 70% of projects fail to deliver their expected benefits [5]. Even when they are partly delivered, they are not fully realised. Reasons for this include the following:

- Project objectives could be focused on cost reduction such that the benefits are not expressed as they can be easily understood and implemented.
- There could be much emphasis on deliverables or outcomes which on their own may not deliver specific benefits.
- Deliverables may lead to the realisation of the benefits over time that is long after the project has been completed. For example, suppose that an electric power generator has just been commissioned in February 2016 and the plant is supposed to generate electricity for the next 10 years. For this to happen, after the project has been completed, facilities should be in place to manage the realisation of the business benefits. However, projects are often erroneously considered finished when their deliverables are completed and accepted, but the benefits of a project are typically generated over time. There may be poor management of its operation during the realisation phase, and often there may not be any prepared facilities with which to manage this key phase. Therefore,

for benefits realisation to work, it is crucial to identify clear benefits (early in the life cycle), and to assign ownership to those responsible for planning and managing their achievement.

■ Central goals of the benefits management process are to bring structure, accountability, clarity and discipline to the definition and delivery of the benefits in projects. It should therefore constitute a key aspect of port-folio management and should start at the earliest stages of the project cycle, well before the approval of the project charter. Effective benefit realisation planning enables organisations to maximise the potential benefits from the investment on the project. Such a planning should also identify and manage the changes that will be required, including managing any resistance that may be encountered.

A Suggested Checklist of Key Components Required for Successful Project Portfolio Management

■ Develop the corporate strategic plan and strategic objectives.
■ Decide and define the benefits and values derivable from each aspect of the plan.
■ Decide on the number of projects and programmes that are required to implement and achieve each benefit. Build a detailed registry of all the projects in the company, ideally in a single database, including name, length, estimated cost, business objective, ROI and business benefits.
■ **Identify how they meet strategic objectives**: This involves compil-ing a list of projects during the annual planning cycle and supporting them with business cases that show estimated costs, ROI, business ben-efit and risk assessment and so on. One of the core criteria on which projects get funded is how closely a project meets the company's strate-gic objectives for the next year.
■ **Prioritise and categorize**: The prioritization process allows the busi-ness to fund the projects that most closely align with your company's strategic objectives. The business then develops evaluation criteria to rank projects in terms of their importance. Establish a set of weighted scoring criteria for the prioritisation of projects. Establish guidelines for determining acceptable risks.
■ Determine the budgets and the organisation's resources that can be invested in the portfolio
■ Implement projects

■ **Monitor, manage and review the portfolio**: The portfolio has to be actively managed and monitored. Many businesses use a centralised Programme Management Office (PMO) or Strategic Implementation Office (SIO) to get financial work progress updates from project leaders. This information goes into a database and is reported to executives via a Project Portfolio Management Team, giving the project inventory and its status. Typically, businesses use a RAG method – Red (Help!), Amber (caution) or green (good) – to identify project status.

■ If projects are planned and run by project teams that are distributed across multiple locations, in order to ensure that each team stays on track with its projects without losing sight of company objectives, controlling the projects becomes increasingly difficult. PPM enables efficient and effective control of company-wide project management such that project teams can plan and control their work while providing a continuous, centralised understanding of progress and performance.

To begin the process of implementing PPM, you might want to broaden your project management goals to focus on the multi-user, role-based environment. Specific objectives could include:

■ Providing the project office with access to dynamic status information that it can use to make timely decisions.

■ Improving efficiency of resource use by properly allocating skilled labour, communicating methodologies and forecasting resource needs more accurately.

■ Improving productivity across the project team as a result of continuous collaboration.

■ Improving communication with all project participants through the use of integrated, organisational-wide systems that put project information on each individual's desktop.

■ Increasing accountability by making consistent, summarised project status information available to top management.

■ Increasing quality and client satisfaction through the use and reuse of best practices.

■ Enabling the maintenance of performance data on completed projects to confirm estimating metrics, generate new or revise existing templates and collect job cost data.

■ Integrating with other business systems to provide a total information system. These goals are specific to project management.

Goal setting: Use best practices from your industry as a guide to setting your goals. Research by the Aberdeen Group has shown that some of the problems encountered by large organisations handling company-wide multiple projects include lack of visibility across the projects. There is some difficulty to understand the costs and resource requirements of many projects. There is also the need to ascertain the level of risks involved in selecting projects. All this information is necessary to ensure that the projects can be properly managed separately and holistically. PPM tools are used to achieve portfolio optimisation through proper selection of the right projects, effective resource allocation, what-if analysis and risk management. The tools include dashboards, scorecards, templates, etc. The Aberdeen research shows that companies using PPM are three times more likely to carry out what-if analyses and use the other tools, and also 50% more likely to conduct profitability analysis. The analysis ensures that projects that are not likely to yield profits are not selected. When a project is selected, it should be managed individually and also added to the portfolio. The portfolio provides a repository of all project information such as costs, risks, timelines, allocation of resources, project requirements, inter-relationship of projects, etc. This ensures that projects are not managed independently in silo but holistically as they affect one another. This ensures that projects are utilised efficiently which make for cost-effectiveness both in lean times when resources are scarce and in normal times. Centralised repository ensures central visibility, enables effective resource allocation and facilitates the use of best practices in project management across all the projects in the enterprise [6].

Questions

1. Why should PPM be necessary in an organisation that is conducting profitable operations and also reaping benefits from their deliverables?
2. Is it necessary to do prioritisation in PPM? If yes, how could it be done?
3. Why is governance necessary in PPM?
4. Is PPM governance different from the organisational governance?

References

1. Harold Balsinger and Michelle Robertson, "Enabling IT governance with project portfolio management," Paper presented at PMI® Global Congress 2004, EMEA, Prague, Czech Republic.

2. PM BokGuide A Guide to the Project Management Body of Knowledge, third edition, Project Management Institute (PMI) (2004), p.17.
3. H. A. Levine, "Project portfolio management: a practical guide to selecting projects, managing portfolios and maximizing benefits", Jossey-Bass, 2005.
4. PPP Governance, http://www.mosaicprojects.com.au/PM-Knowledge_Index. html
5. Standish Group 2015 Chaos Report - Q&A with Jennifer Lynch, https://www. infoq.com/articles/standish-chaos-2015/
6. Aberdeen Group, "Project portfolio management: selecting the right projects for optimal investment opportunity", March 2011.

Chapter 14

Programme Management

Programme management is the process that allows organisations to manage multiple, related projects concurrently to obtain significant benefits from them as a group more than those could be obtained if the projects are managed separately. Many related projects, not managed as a programme, are likely to run off course and fail to achieve the desired outcome. Programme management concentrates on delivering the following:

- New capabilities, products and services
- Benefits and goals
- Strategic objectives
- Change
- Other initiatives

When the business area to be addressed by a programme is identified, a high-level plan, described as the roadmap, is developed.

At the identification stage, a programme usually starts with a vision of a changed organisation and the benefits that will accrue from the change. Delivering the changed organisation will involve coordinating a number of projects and ensuring that their outputs are used to deliver benefits.

Typically, again at the identification stage, the desired benefits are initially identified within a business case that justifies the necessary investment. A detailed specification of the end state of the programme is called a blueprint. However, the scale of programmes and the impact of a dynamic business environment mean that intermittent or regular redefinition may be required.

According to the Association of Project Management (APM), the core programme management processes are:

- **Project coordination:** Identifying, initiating, accelerating, decelerating, redefining and terminating projects within the programme; managing interdependencies between projects, and between projects and business-as-usual activities
- **Transformation:** Taking project outputs and managing change within business-as-usual activities so that outputs deliver outcomes
- **Benefits management:** Defining, quantifying, measuring and monitoring benefits
- **Stakeholder management and communications:** Ensuring that relationships are developed and maintained, thus enabling productive, two-way communication with all key stakeholders

Responsibility for these components lies with three key roles: a programme sponsor, a Programme Manager and Business Change Managers [1].

Programme Goals and Objectives

Goals are clearly defined outcomes and benefits which the programmes are supposed to deliver. Outcomes are the final results, outputs or deliverables realised through the projects, while benefits are the tangible gains and valuable assets to the organisations from the deliverables. For example, a power plant project will deliver a power plant as a deliverable. The benefit will be the electricity that it will generate.

When the plan and objectives of the programme have been defined, individual projects are initiated to achieve the outcomes by their respective Project Managers; the Programme Manager is responsible to ensure that each project is aligned to the programme's goals and benefits in support of the organisation's corporate objectives.

The four stages: The core programme management processes could also be seen as these four stages.

1. Programme identification
2. Programme planning
3. Programme delivery
4. Programme closure

These stages take the programme from identification, then initiation, based on strategy and a desire for change, right through to the final realisation of a defined business objective or benefit.

Programme identification comprises:

- Vision
- Aims and objectives
- Scope

Programme identification comes before the Initiation and the Planning phase: The following are the tasks involved in the initiating phase:

Programme charter: At the initial stage, the programme charter is created with input from the stakeholders. These could include organisational standards such as policies, style guides and branding. The programme charter initiates the programme and its benefits.

High-level programme scope: Here, the objectives of the programme charter are translated into high-level scope statement.

Milestone plan: A high-level milestone plan is created using these objectives and goals. This ensures that the expectations of the stakeholder are aligned with the plan execution.

Accountability matrix: The core team in the execution phase is identified and assigned to roles.

Measurement criteria: Define the measurement criteria for the successful completion of the programme. Stakeholder expectations and requirements are analysed for program success.

Programme kick-off meetings: The last activity in the Initiation and Planning Phase is to initiate programme kick-off meetings with key stakeholders to familiarise the organisation with the programme and to obtain stakeholder buy-in.

Programme Roadmap

It is a chronological and graphical representation of the programme's intended direction and consists of the following:

- It is a documented presentation of each of the goals with a timeline.
- It should show the relationship between the programme activities and its expected benefits.

■ It shows the dependencies between major milestones, the linkages between business strategy and planned prioritised work, and provides high-level view of key milestones and decision points.

Programme planning comprises:

■ Design
■ Approach
■ Resource management
■ Responsibilities

Programme delivery consists of:

■ Monitor and Control
■ Health check
■ Progress reporting
■ Risk and issues management

Programme Closure consists of:

Benefits realisation: It contains other activities as could be seen in the Programme Closure discussed in the next section, which contains guidelines for Managing Successful Programmes (MSPs) [2].

The following section on MSP has been modified and adapted from a publication by the UK Government. It has the title "Guidelines for Managing Programmes, Understanding Programmes and Programme Management," by the UK Department for Business & Innovation Skills (2010) [3]. It is considered necessary to discuss the guidelines because they are recommended following research in public and private papers on the topic.

Managing Successful Programmes

MSP comprises:

1. Principles
2. Governance themes
3. Transformational flow processes

Principles: These are proven, universal principles that apply to all types of programmes and should help to achieve success when used. The seven principles are:

- Remaining aligned with corporate strategy
- Leading change
- Envisioning and communicating a better future
- Focusing on benefits and threat to their achievement
- Designing and delivering a coherent capability
- Learning from experience
- Adding value

Governance themes: The MSP governance themes help one design and implement the control framework through which one delivers changes, achieves outcomes and realises benefits. The nine themes are:

- Organisation
- Vision
- Leadership and Stakeholder Engagement
- Benefits Realisation Management
- Blueprint Design and Delivery
- Planning and Control
- Business Case
- Risk Management and Issue Resolution
- Quality Management

Transformational flow processes consist of

- Identifying the programme process
- Defining the programme process

A programme is a strategic initiative which should be triggered top down by some form of "Mandate" from a Sponsoring Group of senior management, one of whom will serve as the programme's Senior Responsible Owner (SRO).

The "Identifying the Programme" process is used to appoint the SRO who will then define in outline the programme vision, objectives and benefits and record them in a programme brief, which contains an outline business case. This leads to the first key decision by the Sponsoring Group whether or not to commit resources to defining the programme and its management approach in detail, that is whether or not it is sensible and worthwhile to start the Defining a Programme process.

Defining the Programme process is where the Programme Manager and Business Change Manager(s) are appointed. They refine the elements of the brief, build the detailed business case, design governance arrangements, develop the plans, etc. At the end, an important decision is made by the Sponsoring Group whether or not to commit the resources required to carry out the programme and to give the SRO authority to proceed.

If the SRO is given the go-ahead, then work commences on "Managing the Tranches," which is the process where day-to-day governance of the programme is applied by the SRO and Programme Board with involvement of the Sponsoring Group at key points (e.g. Tranche Boundaries). Within each Tranche, changes are implemented to enable the required benefits to be realised. This is achieved by the Programme Manager and Business Change Managers working closely together in:

- Delivering the Capability is the process by which the Programme Manager initiates projects to create outputs and new capability.
- Realising the Benefits is the process which the Business Change Manager(s) use to ensure that the project outputs are properly embedded into "business as usual," the required changes in operational practices and culture are achieved and, as a result, benefits start to be realised and are measured. Eventually there will come a point when the Closing the Programme process is required. This is usually when the whole "blueprint" for change has been delivered and benefits are materialising to a sufficient degree to satisfy the programme's business case.
- Sometimes premature closure will be appropriate if the programme's business case is no longer viable or if programme management no longer adds value. Either way, this leads to the final decision by the Sponsoring Group to close and disband the programme but also to ensure that benefits realisation and measurement continues after the programme has closed.

The main activities at programme closure are:

- Notify stakeholders that the programme is about to close
- Assess the completeness of delivery of the blueprint
- Ensure all projects have completed satisfactorily. If the programme is closing prematurely, then ensure that any existing projects are transferred to relevant business owners.
- Review the performance of the programme
- Identify lessons that may benefit other programmes
- Assess the realisation of benefits to date and, if necessary, hold a final benefits review.

- Update the business case and confirm it has been satisfied
- Allocate responsibility for post-programme reviews of benefits
- Ensure ongoing ownership of any outstanding risks and issues
- Confirm that ongoing operational support arrangements are in place
- Finalise the programme documentation and archive it in accordance with corporate policy
- Disband the programme organisation and hand back resources and support functions

There is a detailed discussion of Programme Benefits Management in Appendix 6.

A Specific Work Success Story

This success story or case study by David Davis has been taken from Projectmanagement.com as an example of the implementation of a programme [4]. It has been reviewed, modified and adapted for publishing in this book.

The challenge: He was assigned as a Programme Manager to implement a major telecommunications e-bonding capability for mobility services to signature customers throughout the world. This was a programme that should provide a repeatable process to help define a customised catalogue of services for each customer and to provide a common interface to performing suppliers that would actually fulfil the orders. For example, a customer may have mobility needs in multiple countries throughout the world, in South America, Asia, Germany, the Netherlands, US, Mexico etc. There might be no common wireless carrier to fulfil all these orders. This was because each country had its own set of rules and data sets that made a single interface impossible to implement.

His role as a Programme Manager involved several different steps as the following:

- Determined and communicated to the key stakeholders in the programme. He was given the task to implement programme management, but there were no formal documents that authorised the programme. Therefore, he created a programme charter and obtained its approval from an executive who signed and emailed it to his peers. This authorised resources to work with him and plan the programme.

Assembled a small team from the product house, operations and IT to create a joint definition of work effort.

■ Shared this document with multiple organisations and was able to assemble a core team of stakeholders and a responsibility matrix.
■ Created a programme plan which defined various work packages and the agreed time duration for certain deliverables. Among these deliverables were a business requirements document, benefits realisation plan and a governance model.
■ Developed the following seven project charters to implement the work efforts:
  – Three charters were specific to IT development.
  – One charter was to the marketing and technical implementation plan.
  – Two charters were specific to process and life cycle support.
  – One charter was for developing a repeatable process for catalogue management.
■ Prepared the cost of the projects using a high-level order magnitude to a benefits realisation plan.
■ Established the expectations for the deliverables.

In summary, his procedure was as follows:

■ He started his planning processes by making sure he brought in owners and executive sponsorship of the programme from the business.
■ He produced a programme charter that authorised organisations to commit resources to the planning.
■ He prepared the roadmap and the business realisation plans.
■ He issued a programme plan which outlined how work package was aligned which then was used to generate a charter for each project to help meet those objectives.
■ Once the charters were defined respective Project Managers were assigned for implementing the requirements of the work.

Tools and techniques: Those used in this planning process were as follows:

■ Constant communication and dialogue with key stakeholders and a small work team
■ Interacting with knowledge workers through facilitating meetings with different organisation to define business rules and programme requirements

- Baselining documents and using the concept of progressive elaboration to monitor control of their evolution from a planning cycle until project implementation
- Interacting with the teams through a defined governance model so that all organisations knew the protocol for handling issues, communicating status and reporting task completion.

Questions

1. What is a programme?
2. Why is programme management necessary?
3. What are the phases of programme management?
4. How do you ensure that the benefits derived from the programme will be harvested?

References

1. "Association of project management body of knowledge," https://www.apm .org.uk/body-of-knowledge/context/governance/programme-management/
2. Duncan Haughey, "A framework for programme management", *Programme Management*, 28 September 2009.
3. "Guidelines for managing programmes, understanding programmes and programme management," UK Department for Business & Innovation Skills, 2010.
4. David Davis, "A specific work success story," written in 2009 and published in the Benefits Realization Blog, 06 August 2016, Projectmanagement.com

Chapter 15

Project Management Life Cycle

This is not a full course on project management. Its objective is to help the user acquire a clear understanding of the project management life cycle.

Project management life cycle: We shall first review its definition. It is defined as the stages that one has to go through to *manage* the project. According to the PMBOK Guide, it comprises the following process groups:

1. **Initiating Process Group:** This defines and authorises the project or a project phase.
2. **Planning Process Group:** This defines and refines objectives and plans the course of action required to attain the objectives and scope that the project was undertaken to address.
3. **Executing Process Group:** This integrates people and other resources to implement the project management plan for the project.
4. **Monitoring and Controlling Process Group:** This regularly measures and monitors progress to identify variances from the project management plan so that corrective action can be taken when necessary to meet project objectives.
5. **Closing Process Group:** This formalises acceptance of the product, service or result, and brings the project or project phase to an orderly end.

The Project management life cycle can also be described as the processes for achieving set goals or objectives within the constraint of time, budget and staffing restrictions.

The Process Groups

Introduction: We shall study the processes in each process group, starting with the Initiating Process Group. However, before this, we need to take note of some pre-initiating activities.

Pre-initiating activities

These have to be completed before the Initiating Process. They include the following:

- Identifying and documenting the business needs of the organisation.
- There may be need for a feasibility study to determine if the project will be profitable.
- Development of clear descriptions of the project objectives. This should contain the following documents:
  - A description of the project scope – that is the extent of the project.
  - The project deliverables.
  - The project duration.
- A forecast of the resources that could be used.

Initiating Process Group

Definition: This is the process group for an official authorisation of the commencement of the project and definition of its scope.

Description

This is a process that facilitates the formal authorisation to start a new project or a project phase. Some of the activities are often done external to the project's scope of control by the organisation.

Activities of the Initiating Process Group

The activities in this process group include the following:

1. A clear description of the project objectives is developed in this process.
2. Reasons why a specific project among others is chosen is made known at this level.

3. Basic description of the project scope is done at this level, thereby showing:
   - The deliverables.
   - Project duration start date and estimated finish date.
   - A forecast of the resources for the organisation's investment analysis.
   - Having selected a project before now, the project selection process is made known here.

Explanation

The Initiating Process is the first phase of the project. Prior to formal work on this phase, that is during the pre-initiating phase, a business problem (or opportunity) is identified and a business case which provides various solution options is defined. A feasibility study could be conducted to investigate the likelihood of each solution option addressing the business problem and a final recommended cost-effective solution is put forward. Once the recommended solution is approved, a project is initiated to deliver the approved solution. A Project Manager is appointed in this process. The Project Manager begins recruiting a project team and establishes a project office environment. The main processes in the Initiating Process Group include the following:

- **Develop project charter**: The Charter outlines the objectives, scope and structure of the new project
- Develop preliminary project scope statement

Develop Project Charter

Definition:

Project charter is a document that officially starts a project and could be described as follows:

Description:

- It is usually signed by the performing organisation's senior management.
- It names the Project Manager and gives him or her the authority to direct the project.
- It includes high-level project requirements.
- It contains a summary-level, preliminary project budget.

■ It outlines the objectives, scope and structure of the new project.
■ It authorises the Project Manager to begin recruiting a project team and to establish a Project Office environment.
■ Approval is then sought to move into the detailed planning phase.
■ In multi-phase projects, this process is used to validate or refine the decisions made during the previous develop charter process.

Explanation:

Project charter is one of the most important documents of a project because it contains the authority for creating projects. If you do not have a project charter, then you do not have an official project or the authority to create a project. The following documents have to be available as inputs to the process of developing the charter. They include:

■ The contract for the project, if it is being contracted.
■ Project statement of work: This is a description of the deliverables whether services or products that will result from the project. For an internal project, the project sponsor will provide the statement of work. For an external project, the customer will provide it as a part of a bid document such as a request for proposal (RFP), a request for information (RFI) and a request for bid (RFB).

Develop Preliminary Project Scope Statement

This process, with the use of the project charter and other inputs, produces preliminary high-level definitions of a project. It addresses and documents the following:

■ Project and product objectives.
■ Product or service requirements and characteristics.
■ Product acceptance criteria.
■ Project boundaries.
■ Project requirements and deliverables.
■ Project constraints.
■ Project assumptions.
■ Initial project organisation.
■ Initial defined risks.
■ Schedule milestones.
■ Initial WBS.

- Order of magnitude cost estimate: This estimate is in the range of –25% to +75% from actual.
- Project configuration management requirements: It is a collection of formal documented procedures used for many functions such as to identify and document the functional and physical characteristics of a product, result, service or component; control and record any changes to such characteristics; etc.
- Approval requirements.

Explanation:

It is developed by the project management team from information provided by the initiator or sponsor. In summary, it defines what needs to be accomplished in the project. It addresses and documents the characteristics and boundaries of the project, its associated products and services, the methods of acceptance and scope control.

Planning Process Group

Definition:

This is the group in which all the detailed planning is done for the successful completion of a project. The planning group obtains information from many sources with which it identifies, defines and matures the project scope, project cost, schedules of project activities, relationships and resources arrangements. The detailed planning phase involves the development of the project management plan by the creation of its constituent subsidiary plans.

Develop Project Management Plan

This is the process where definition, preparation, integration and coordination of all subsidiary plans are made. This makes project management plan the primary source of information for how the project will be properly executed, monitored, controlled and closed. The project planning can be achieved by carrying out the following steps and actions on processes which are subsidiaries or components of the project management plan.

Scope Planning

The scope planning is for creating a project scope management. This documents how the project scope will be defined, controlled and verified. Note that how the scope is defined is determined by the importance of the project. A critical project will require formal, thorough and time-intensive definition, while a routine project will require less documentation and scrutiny. The breaking down of the scope into work breakdown structure is also done. With this the scope of project should be properly managed.

Scope Definition

The definition is now prepared in line with how the scope should be defined as stated in step one. This results in a detailed project scope statement as a basis for future decision. For example, the needs, wants and expectations of the stakeholders are analysed and converted into project requirements.

Create Work Breakdown Structure

At this level, major project deliverables and project work are subdivided into smaller, more manageable components. The components can be used to view the deliverables of the project since the decomposition of the work to achieve the objectives that will create the required deliverables that cover the total scope of the project. The essence of the breakdown or decomposition is to arrive at manageable work packages. The work packages are identified and listed in WBS Dictionary. Work packages are at the lowest level of each branch of the work breakdown structure. This brings about precision and accuracy in the implementation to produce the project deliverables.

Activity Definition

Work packages are the deliverables at the lowest level of work breakdown structure (WBS). Work packages are further decomposed into smaller components called schedule activities which provide a basis for estimating, scheduling, executing and monitoring and controlling the project work. Identification of specific activities that need to be performed to produce the various project deliverables is done at this level. In other words, the various activities that will be performed in the project will be itemised.

Activity Sequencing

This is placing the activities in the order that they will be performed, that is to determine and place the activity which should be performed before the other. In effect it is used to establish and implement relationships between the activities.

Activity Resource Estimating

This is estimating the quantities of the resources required to perform each schedule activity, as well as the type of resources required for each activity. By resources, we mean human, material and equipment.

Activity Duration Estimating

This process involves estimating the number of work periods or the duration needed to perform each individual schedule activity. It could be in hours, days, weeks or months.

Schedule Development

This is the analysis of activity sequences, duration, resources requirements and schedule constraints and this information is used to create the project schedule. Thus, for each activity using the activity duration estimate, we can determine its planned start and finish dates. Note that this information can change as the process is iterative, changing accordingly as more information is obtained.

Cost Estimating

This is the process for developing an approximation of the costs of the resources needed for the successful start and completion of the project activities.

Cost Budgeting

This is the process for summing up or aggregating the estimated costs of individual activities to establish the cost of the project. The first budget prepared when the project is approved is used to establish the cost baseline, and it is used to monitor subsequent changes in the budget.

Quality Planning

It is the identification of the quality standards relevant to the project and how to implement them in the entire project.

Human Resources Planning

This process is used for identifying roles, responsibilities and reporting relationships between the labour resources and creating staff management plan.

Communication Planning

This communication planning involves determining the information and communication needs of the project stakeholders.

Risk Planning

This is the process for highlighting potential risks in the project and actions that should be taken to mitigate threats and enhance opportunities.

Plan Purchases and Acquisitions

This is the process of determining what to purchase (material, labour and other things) or acquire, and when and how and it should be done. The acquisition could be from external sources.

Plan Contracting

This process involves planning and documenting requirements for products and services, and their potential sellers.

Project Execution Process Group

This process group does the execution of each activity and task listed in the project plan. It is typically the longest phase and the costliest in the project (in terms of duration). It is the phase within which the deliverables are physically constructed. The actual activities undertaken to construct each deliverable will vary, depending on the type of project (e.g. engineering, building development, computer infrastructure or business process re-engineering projects). Deliverables may be constructed in a "waterfall" fashion (where each activity is undertaken in sequence until the deliverable is finished) or an "iterative" fashion (where iterations of each deliverable are constructed until the deliverable meets the requirements of the customer).

This process group deals with coordinating people and resources, integrating and performing projects' activities in accordance to the project management plan.

To ensure that the customer's requirements are met, the Project Manager monitors and controls the activities, resources and expenditure required to build each deliverable throughout the execution phase. While the activities and tasks are being executed, a series of management processes are undertaken to monitor and control the deliverables which are the outputs of the project. These should be employed to ensure that the quality of the final deliverable meets the acceptance criteria set by the customer. A number of management processes are also undertaken to ensure that the project proceeds as planned. These include the following:

- Identification of changes, risks and issues; the review of deliverable quality; and the measurement of each deliverable being produced against the acceptance criteria.
- The Project Manager works with the project team as he or she directs the performance of the planned activities. The Project Manager also manages the various technical and organisational interfaces that exist within the project.
- It may be necessary to employ and train more project team members.
- The team will implement the planned methods and standards: create, control, verify and validate project deliverables.
- The Project Managers manage risks and implement risk response activities.
- They implement any approved changes on project's scope, plans and environment.
- They manage and monitor and contractors working on the project.
- They establish and manage communication channels both external and internal to the project team.
- They collect work performance information on the status of the deliverables and report to stakeholders.
- Information should include cost, schedule, technical and quality progress and status information to facilitate forecasting.
- They will collect, document lessons learned and implement approved process improvement activities.

Monitoring and Controlling Process Group

Description:

This process group is concerned with monitoring all processes associated with initiating, planning, executing and closing of the project. With these processes, problems of the project will be identified timely and corrected. It involves watching, checking and correcting project activities. Monitoring is performed throughout the project. It includes collecting, measuring and disseminating performance information; assessing measurements and trends; and effecting improvements. Continuous monitoring gives the team insight into the health of the project and identifies areas that require special attention.

Status reporting, progress measurements and forecasting are all involved in monitoring. Performance reports provide information on the project's performance with respect to scope, cost, quality, resources and risk.

Monitoring and Controlling Project Work Process Group conducts the following functions:

It compares actual performance against the project management plan.

It assesses performance to determine whether any corrective or preventive actions are necessary; if yes, it recommends them.

Risk monitoring is done to ensure the early identification of risk, status report and appropriate risk plan executed.

This group provides information for status reporting, measurement and forecasting of progress.

It monitors the implementation of approved changes when and as they occur.

In short, it enables the comparison of actual project performance against all the plans made in the components of the project management plan. They include comparing actual cost with planned-in cost, quality, etc.

Integrated Change Control Process

This also belongs to the Monitoring and Controlling Process Group. The objective is to control factors that create changes. It is performed from project initiation to completion. Change control is necessary because projects hardly perform as planned in the project management plan. As a result, the project management plan, the project scope statement and the deliverables must be successfully delivered by carefully and continuously managing changes by rejecting or approving the changes. Approved changes are added to the revised plan to be implemented, that is the baseline. It is clear that the changes are controlled in such a way that their effects are beneficial. The change control includes the following change management activities:

■ Identifying that a change has occurred or needs to occur
■ Influencing the factors that affect integrated change control so that only approved changes are implemented
■ Reviewing and approving requested changes, all recommended corrective and preventive actions
■ Managing the approved changes as they occur, by regulating the flow of requested changes
■ Maintaining the integrity of baselines by releasing only approved changes for incorporation into project products or services and also maintaining related configuration and planning documentation
■ Controlling and updating the scope, cost, budget, schedule and quality requirements based upon approved changes, by coordinating changes across the entire project

Close Project Process

The Close Project Process is used to terminate officially or formally all activities of a project or a project phase, transfer the completed product to others or close a cancelled project. It is used for finalising all activities across all of the process groups to formally close the project or a project phase. It is also used to perform the following functions:

■ It establishes the procedures to coordinate activities needed to verify and document the project variables.
■ It coordinates procedures required to formalise the acceptance of those deliverables by the customer or sponsor.
■ It provides procedures to investigate and document the reasons for actions taken if a project is terminated or cancelled.
   There are two procedures in the Close Project Process, namely the Administrative Closure and Contract Closure Procedures.

Administrative Closure

Two functions are performed in this Closure, they are:

■ It details all the activities, interactions, roles and responsibilities of the project team members and other stakeholders involved in performing the administrative closure procedure.
■ It includes integrated activities needed to collect project records, analyse project success or failure, gather lessons learned and archive project information for future use by the organisation.

Contract Closure

This procedure includes all activities and interactions needed to settle and close any contract agreement established for the project. It also includes those related activities supporting the administrative closure and others such as:

■ It involves product verification for all contracted assignments completed correctly and satisfactorily. It also involves administrative closure in the form of updating contract records to reflect the final results and archiving the information for future use.
■ It also includes terms for completing and settling each contract, including the resolution of any open item, and closing each contract applicable to the project or a project phase.
■ If a contract was entered into, the contract terms and conditions can also prescribe specifications for contract closure that must be part of this procedure.

Questions

1. Why is a project charter necessary?
2. Why should the project team not go on straight to execution and bypass planning?
3. What is the importance of monitoring and control?
4. We discussed project performance management: where should it fit with the project management life cycle?
5. In which phase does lessons learned occur? Is it really necessary to discuss it; if yes, why is it important?

Chapter 16

Transitioning from Project to Operations and Maintenance

An important aspect of success and sustainability of project deliverables is their operation and maintenance. This is necessary to enable the benefits and values of the deliverables to be harvested.

Organisations often have multiple project deliverables to release to customers and business units. Often project teams become lost in transition when the deliverables are not properly transitioned to appropriate operation support teams. The problem is such that the project teams continue to work to release the next deliverable while it has not been possible to organise adequate support for released deliverables. Therefore, in the absence of properly defined operational roles and responsibilities, project teams endanger future deliverable releases and also suffer from role confusion. This could be avoided if the project team included operations support planning and transition early on in the project planning and schedule development.

(Much of the materials for this topic has been adapted and modified from a publication by Andrew Makar as acknowledged in Reference 1.)

Some guidelines to achieve smooth transition of the deliverables from project to operations and governance include the following:

- **Deliverable description:** Provide a high-level description of the deliverable(s) or service(s) to be maintained and the scope of post-implementation operations and maintenance activities.
- **Budget:** Identify the budget associated with post-implementation operations and maintenance activities.

■ **Roles and responsibilities:** Specify the roles and responsibilities associated with post-implementation operations and maintenance as well as the skill sets needed to perform those functions. Roles to identify include the primary business contact, post-implementation operations and maintenance team lead(s), key technical staff, customer or help desk support, documentation, training and other support staff.

■ **Performance measures and reporting:** Identify critical performance measures for maintenance activities and for product or service performance. Include information on how measures will be captured and reported.

■ **Management approach:** Identify new or refer to existing methodologies for establishing maintenance priorities and other change management strategies.

■ **Customer/business owner management:** Describe how stakeholder/ customers will be involved in or informed about post-implementation operations and maintenance activities. Describe key stakeholders and methods for communicating with them.

■ **Standard operation and business practices:** Identify methodologies, processes and tools used for change control and configuration management, problem report management, customer support strategy, life cycle testing, risk identification and mitigation, data sharing practices, storage, disaster recovery, security, customer support strategies, etc.

■ **Documentation strategies:** Describe new or refer to existing documentation standards and expectations. Include descriptions of routine documentation, such as reports and user, usage, problem and change information, as well as product/service documentation. Include details on where documentation is stored and how it is accessed.

■ **Training:** Describe ongoing post-implementation training activities.

■ **Acceptance:** Define the time when the project staff and maintenance staff agree that implementation and transition activities are complete and maintenance activities may begin.

■ **Operations status meeting with business partners and IT stakeholders:** Initiate an operations status meeting which includes business partners and IT management to review jointly the health and performance of the application.

■ **Meeting on production issues and incidents with business subject matter experts and the technical team:** Start a separate meeting to review incidents, production and immediate support issues. This will ensure that different teams are handling project and production issues and will help eliminate any confusion of roles that may arise.

■ **A change control board to manage changes in operations:** As business needs change, new reports, fields, interfaces and customer interactions become necessary. With a change control board, customers can request changes to their projects without any interference to the project team.

■ **Governance arrangement should be communicated to project stakeholders:** The model presents information on how issues, changes and operations review are handled. This information should be communicated to all business and technical stakeholders as soon as it has been obtained. This should minimise disruption in project and operations activities.

Mutual knowledge transfer between project and operations teams:

■ **Provide knowledge transfer between project and support teams:** There should be effective communication between the two teams. Moreover, the project schedule should contain transition documentation tasks to communicate the processes and procedures required for application support. Other items of information include help desk coordination, escalation contacts, potential and existing problems and their solutions and disaster recovery procedures.

Maintenance: For each project the following information needs to be considered in maintenance:

■ Satisfactory maintenance and replacement requirements for various parts, components and equipment at different stages of construction and production need to be identified and planned for.

■ Maintenance requirements should be assessed in terms of both the maintenance equipment that may be necessary for the efficient maintenance of the plant and facilities and the maintenance skills and capability that need to be developed.

■ The development of maintenance skills and capability is of particular importance, especially in developing countries where efficient maintenance may be both more difficult and more important because of difficulties in obtaining replacements. Such skills should be developed, through training programmes at the project implementation stage, for general-purpose maintenance and with respect to maintenance of specific, complex equipment and facilities.

■ Replacement requirements need to be determined for wear-and-tear parts, tools, jigs and fixtures in engineering-goods industries, and, for spare parts, components and materials for plant, buildings and other facilities in all projects.

■ An efficient balance has to be maintained between replacement requirements and stocks of parts, components and materials. Such a balance constitutes a critical feature of financial planning of inventories during the project implementation stage.

■ Inventory requirements for maintenance and replacement items will vary with each project and depend on the nature of the project, the extent of utilisation of particular parts or materials and the speed with which such items can be replaced. In several fields, fairly standard stock levels are prescribed for various maintenance and replacement items. These may, however, need to be adjusted in situations where such items have to be imported, and there are foreign exchange constraints. Estimates should be prepared in this regard and incorporated in the factory cost estimates.

■ Study and list maintenance planning needs and tasks. These should include human and material resources and costs associated with maintenance, both inhouse and outsourced.

■ Design timelines for developing and implementing maintenance plan components including persons responsible for various aspects of maintenance such as support strategy, change management strategies, administration and miscellaneous issues.

Questions

1. Why is it necessary to achieve a smooth transition from project to operations?
2. What arrangement should be in place to ensure that the deliverables are kept in operation after the project team completes its assignments and leaves the site?
3. In the maintenance and operation of your project deliverables, what do you expect to be the essential resources to be available after the take-over for operations?

4. Can you identify the sources of the material resources necessary for the operation of the deliverables? Are these local or overseas; do the fund exist for their procurement?

Reference

1. Andrew Makar, "Project transition to operations, transition" – h koppdelaney (Flickr.com). Tactical project management, https://www.tacticalprojectman agement.com/project-transition-to-operations/

SECTION 5

SUMMARY OF SUGGESTIONS FOR THE ACHIEVEMENT OF SUCCESS AND SUSTAINABILITY IN PROJECT DELIVERY

5

Some of the contributions made in this book for the achievement of success and sustainability in project delivery and a tabular guideline for the use of the suggested framework are presented in this chapter.

It needs to be re-emphasised that success means that projects are completed not only to deliver outputs in time, on cost and with quality but also that positive, measurable benefits have been delivered to the stakeholders. This success includes the fact that the deliverables are operated and maintained within the planned lifetime to provide the benefits that necessitated the initiation and implementation of the projects. This is the thrust of the contributions of this book.

In the next chapter, a brief review of the steps that an organisation needs to take to actualise this success is summarised.

Chapter 17

Contributions of the Book for the Achievement of Success and Sustainability in Project Delivery

The contributions include the following:

- Reasons for failures discussed with suggestions on how to avoid them.
- Circles of causes of project failures and abandonment, circles of corruption and circles of failed governance are used to summarise and define the problems that need to be solved.
- Suggestion on the necessity for a structured approach for the solution of the problems and project delivery. For example, using a framework containing vision, mission and strategic objectives include the estimated financial returns from the deliverables need to be planned for public and government projects and programmes intended for commercial operations. In other words, for a new project that will produce deliverables for commercial operation, there should be a plan of how the deliverables will be supported in operations. There should be an estimate of how much benefit and returns will be produced by the deliverable and when.
- The framework also contains OPM consisting of PMOs, Portfolio Management, Programme Management and Project Management and

Table 17.1   A Tabular Guideline for the Use of the Recommended Framework

S/No.	Topic Description	Chapter
1	Vision and mission: Prepare the vision and mission statements	12
2	Strategy: Write the strategy statement	12
3	Objectives: Prepare the strategic objectives	12
4	OPM: Start OPM	13
5	EPMO: Establish an enterprise PMO	13
6	PPM: Start PPM	13
7	Prepare the initiatives, projects, programmes and deliverables in operations	13
8	Governance	13
9	Selection and prioritisation of projects and deliverables in operations	13
10	Programme management: Implement programmes	14
11	Benefit planning and project grouping into programmes	14
12	PM: Implement projects	15
13	Transitioning: Implement the transition of the project to operation and maintenance	16
14	Prepare new projects and revise current projects and project deliverables in operation and maintenance	Not discussed separately
15	Implement the operation and maintenance schemes	Not discussed separately
16	Revert to numbers 6 and 7 in this guideline and continue the cycle	

how to implement them. These provide the processes through which the vision, mission and strategic objectives can be implemented.

■ Suggestions on benefit planning and management. This should include a timeline for the benefit to be produced and the quantity and value of the benefit. It should also explain how the benefit so produced and converted into financial terms could be reinvested in the organisation and for the operation of the deliverable. These points have to be planned for and agreed to even before the project is started.

- Guidelines on transitioning from project management to the operation and maintenance of project deliverables.
- **Prerequisite:** A board of directors should be in place from the onset.

Tabular Guideline for the Use of the Recommended Framework

This is presented in Table 17.1.

APPENDICES

Appendix 1: National Project Management Office (NPMO)

There is a necessity to establish a unit, a National Project Management Office (NPMO) charged with the responsibility of end-to-end project management in African countries. It should be empowered to participate with government departments and ministries in discussion and investments in future major projects. No ministry should procure projects for the country independently.

The responsibilities of the NPMO could include the following:

- Empowered to analyse and participate in negotiation of all new national projects
- Work for the sustainability of appropriate projects
- Authorised to monitor and eliminate unviable projects
- Recommend and implement effective project management methodologies and best practices in project management
- Supervise and organise the training of Nigerian project managers and team members

A View of Project Management Practice in Advanced Countries

Research shows that important national projects are not abandoned in advanced countries and developed economies when an election is imminent or is being conducted. In order to eliminate this unacceptable behaviour which is a reflection of our failure to plan and underlines the underdevelopment of our economy and its programme management, it may be wise to examine and learn from the practices in three developed economies as discussed next.

Programme Management in the UK, Canada and the US

Practice in the UK Government

The UK Government established the Major Projects Authority (MPA), which works with the Treasury and other government departments to provide independent assurance on major projects. It also supports colleagues across departments to build skills and improve the way to manage and deliver projects. The MPA is part of the Efficiency and Reform Group in the Cabinet Office. The MPA has a clear and enforceable mandate to do the following:

■ Draw up the Government Major Projects Portfolio
■ Request, review and approve integrated assurance and approval plans for each major project or programme
■ Carry out assurance reviews where there is a cause for concern
■ Intervene directly, where appropriate, in the delivery of major projects that are failing by providing commercial and operational support
■ Work with departments to build skills and expertise in projects and programme management
■ Publish an annual report on major projects

On 1 January 2016 the MPA merged with Infrastructure UK to form a new organisation called the Infrastructure and Projects Authority

Practice in the Canadian Government

The Canadian Government created a Major Projects Management Office (MPMO). It is an organisation whose role is to "provide overarching project management and accountability for major resource projects in the federal regulatory review process, and to facilitate improvements to the regulatory system for major resource projects."

Its other activities are as follows:

■ It provides guidance to project proponents and other stakeholders.
■ It coordinates project agreements and timelines between federal departments and agencies.

- It tracks and monitors the progression of major resource projects through the federal regulatory review process.
- It also investigates and identifies short- and longer-term solutions to improve the performance of the federal environmental assessment and regulatory process for major resource projects.

Practice in the US Government

One of the programme management offices in the US Government is the Project Management Coordination Office (PMCO). Some of its functions are as follows:

- It provides guidance, leadership, training and tools in programme and project management to Office of Energy Efficiency and Renewable Energy (EERE) Headquarters and field employees.
- It is an internal business operations office with a mission to provide EERE executive managers, line managers and staff offices the unified corporate tools, products and services that enable EERE to ensure the highest value return on its research, development and deployment investment at the lowest realistic risk.
- It leads the development of policies, processes and reporting for project and risk management, including Funding Opportunity Announcement and Active Project Management (APM), and leads the development of policies for Annual Operating Plans (AOPs).
- It also manages the governance and Change Control Board processes, tools, support and our online resource centre, PM Central.
- It provides oversight and risk management of the EERE project portfolio, including base-funded, Recovery Act and Congressionally Directed Projects.
- It works with the Workforce Management Office to provide project and risk management training and certification support.

Case for a National Programme Management Office

With the benefit of the information provided in the foregoing paragraphs, it is justifiable to recommend the establishment of a National Programme Management Office. Its functions in the immediate, medium to long term, could include the following:

Immediate functions:

- Draw up a comprehensive list of all approved national government projects specifying their completion status, costs and resource requirements
- Track and monitor the progress of major projects biweekly or as frequently as desired
- Improve communication and collaboration between contractors and government
- Manage the governance, amendment, variation and change control processes
- Draw up a list of the various contractors and their performance history in the various projects in the country
- Coordinate project agreements and timelines between federal departments and contractors

Medium to long-term functions:

- Work with departments to build skills and expertise in projects and programme management
- Provide guidance to project proponents and other stakeholders
- Intervene directly, where appropriate, in the delivery of major projects that are failing by providing commercial and operational support
- Investigate and identify short- and longer-term solutions to improve the performance of projects
- Provide guidance, leadership, training and tools in programme and project management
- Lead the development of policies, processes and reporting for project and risk management
- Provide project and risk management training and certification support
- Implement project governance and processes
- Improve and introduce consistent reporting
- Improve management and control of resources
- Mentor and build capacity for all project team members

Appendix 2: Definitions and Explanations for Frequently Used Project Management Words for Busy Executives and Managers in Developing Countries

Introduction

On every working day, many managers take decisions on projects with budgets running into millions of pounds and dollars. Most of these managers do not understand what a project is or the project life cycle or even how to manage a project. What they understand is that the project has been awarded to a company for a given sum and that the management of the company has undertaken to complete the project within the time frame. The company may have a track record of doing projects. But can they deliver? Can they produce the agreed deliverables on this project within the agreed time and on budget?

The approving manager does not know. It is inexcusable that a manager is happily and frequently approving multimillion pounds projects without any clue as to what are involved in doing them.

No one should be blamed for being ignorant of how to manage a project. The blame is for being ignorant and doing NOTHING to improve one's skills and knowledge base.

It is incorrect for one to be managing what one does not understand. Such managers are doing a disservice to their organisation, to the nation and most importantly to themselves. This is one of the reasons why our country, Nigeria, has an industrial landscape littered with uncompleted and abandoned projects even with all the money paid up.

Why Ignorance Persists

1. **Absence of relevant continuing education**

    Most managers can justifiably claim that they have more than 10 to 15 years' experience in their organisations. They may be the longest serving graduates. However, they have no skills of modern technology or structured project management. The continuing education programme approved for the organisation does not cover such subjects. Indeed, the programme is irrelevant in the light of present-day project management challenges in project delivery.

2. **Failure to do continuous professional development**

    It is unfortunately the case that, in most developing countries, especially in sub-Saharan Africa, most graduates and professionals do not continue with their professional development. They relax and do nothing about it. This is not the case in advanced nations where professional development is a life-long practice. As a result, our managers fail to develop themselves.

Definitions of basic project management terms

We shall discuss the definitions of the following terms:

■ Project
■ Project Life Cycle
■ Project Management
■ Project Management Body of Knowledge (PMBOK)
■ Project Management Information System
■ Project Management Life Cycle
■ Project Management Methodology
■ Programme
■ Portfolio

- Process
- Sponsor
- Stakeholder
- Triple Constraint
- Project Management Office
- RFP
- RFI

We shall add the following definitions:

1. **Project Management** is the application of knowledge, skills, tools and techniques to project activities in order to achieve the desired goals and meet project requirements.
2. **Guide to the Project Management Body of Knowledge (PMBOK Guide):** This is the guide that describes the sum of knowledge, prepared by the PMI, within the profession of project management. It includes proven professional practices and innovative practices emerging in the profession, both published and unpublished. The PMBOK is constantly evolving.
3. **Project Management Information System (PMIS):** An information system comprising tools and techniques for gathering, integrating and disseminating the outputs of project management processes. It can include both manual and automated systems and is used to support all aspects of the project from initiating, through to closing.
4. **Project Management Methodology:** This is a set of strategic procedures or guidelines produced by a vendor for implementing project management processes. Each vendor produces its own peculiar and probably patented procedures through which the processes, from initiating to closing, of project management can be implemented. For example, Primavera P6 is a methodology of Primavera.
5. **Portfolio:** A collection of projects or programmes of an organisation that are grouped together to facilitate the effective management of their activities to meet organisational strategic objectives. Note that a collection of related projects constitutes a programme and a collection of related programmes constitutes a portfolio.
6. **PMO (Project Management Office):** This is a unit in an organisation assigned with various responsibilities related to the coordination of projects: training, development and deployment of project professionals, etc. The responsibilities of a PMO can include support functions to project

teams, recommendation of software packages for enterprise-wide usage, advising top management on project issues and even direct management of some critical and strategic projects.

7. **RFI (Request for Information):** It is a standard business procedure aimed at collecting information about the capabilities of various suppliers.

8. **RFP (Request for Proposal):** It is a procurement procedure used to request proposals from prospective sellers of services or products such as contractors or vendors.

9. **RFQ (Request for Quotation):** It is also a type of procurement procedure used for requesting price quotations from prospective sellers of products or services. The sellers could be contractors or vendors. It also could be used to invite the sellers to submit bid on a product or service that they should supply (template).

Appendix 3: KPI-BSC Link

The linkage of KPIs to strategic objectives is a pillar for effective reporting and monitoring of performance. PricewaterhouseCoopers (PwC) reported that some of their executives monitored 34 FTSE 350 companies for their use of KPIs. Sixteen of them linked their KPIs to strategic objectives. Eleven of these linked one KPI to one strategic objective, and the relevance of the linkage was clear. The other five linked one KPI to more than one strategic objective, and their relevance was less clear. It is also the case that where the KPIs are easily measured, data is always available for internal management use and also to meet external requirements, including regulatory obligations. The Financial Reporting Council's (FRC) Guidance on strategic reporting states: "The KPIs used in analysis should be those that the directors consider most effective in assessing progress against objectives or strategy, monitoring principal risks, or otherwise use to measure the development, performance and position of the entity."

Reference: "Measuring Performance, KPIs and the Link to Strategic Objectives," www.pwc.co.uk/corporate reporting

Selecting the right KPIs will depend on what is to be tracked. Each department will use different KPI types to measure success based on specific business goals and targets.

KPI Reports and Dashboards

To be useful, KPIs need to be monitored and reported on; if they change in real time, they should be monitored in real time. Dashboards are the perfect tool for KPI reports as they can be used to show the performance of an enterprise, a specific department or a key business operation.

Measuring and monitoring business performance is critical, but focusing on the wrong key performance indicators can be detrimental. So can be poorly structured KPIs, or KPIs that are too difficult, or costly to, obtain or to monitor on a regular basis.

Tracking your KPIs is one thing, but to ensure they are being used to achieve your business goals, they need to be related to and generate action. Tracking and reporting on a KPI each week or month, as necessary, is useful as it brings information that helps direct action to keep the measured value on track with the goal.

BSC and KPI

An essential function of key performance indicators and a balanced scorecard is to align organisational performance with the long-term strategic objectives of the company. When used in monitoring and measurements, the key performance indicators help determine if the performance of the organisation is moving in the right direction.

The following are the four basic viewpoints or perspectives to take with respect to the KPI balanced scorecard linkage:

1. **Financial perspective – tracking financial performance:** This perspective views organisational financial performance and the use of financial resources.
2. **Customer/stakeholder perspective:** This perspective views organisational performance from the point of view of the customer or other key stakeholders that the organisation is designed to serve, tracking customer satisfaction, attitudes and market share goals.
3. **Internal process perspective:** It views organisational performance through the lenses of the quality and efficiency related to our product or services or other key business processes. It covers internal operational goals needed to meet customer objectives.
4. **The learning and growth or innovation perspective or organisational capacity:** It views organisational performance through the lenses of human capital, infrastructure, technology, culture and other capacities that are key to breakthrough performance. It views intangible drivers for future success such as human capital, organisational capital, training, informational systems, etc.

The idea is that these four perspectives are interdependent and hierarchical as described in the following paragraphs. Growth is driven by constant learning and innovation, which leads to the refinement of internal processes. The improvement in internal processes through the KPI balanced scorecard helps drive increases in operating efficiency, which result in higher customer satisfaction and increased financial performance.

In effect, the BSC connects the big picture strategy elements such as mission (our purpose), vision (what we aspire for), core values (what we believe in), strategic focus areas (themes, results and/or goals) and the more operational elements such as objectives (continuous improvement activities), measures (or key performance indicators, or KPIs, which track strategic performance), targets (our desired level of performance) and initiatives (projects that help achieve the targets).

Other notes on the balanced scorecard such as Strategic Mapping are given in Appendix 8. Suffice it however to summarise the necessity of the balanced scorecards here as follows.

While traditionally companies used only short-term financial performance to measure success, the "balanced scorecard" has included additional non-financial strategic measures to the system in order to focus better on long-term success. The system has evolved over the years into a fully integrated strategic management system.

Recognising some of the weaknesses and vagueness of previous management approaches, the balanced scorecard approach provides a clear recommendation of what companies should measure in order to "balance" the financial perspective.

The balanced scorecard depicts traditional financial measures which show past events were before acceptable as adequate information for companies for which investments in long-term capabilities and customer relationships were not critical for success. However, these financial measures are no longer adequate to guide companies to forecast and create values through investment in stakeholders such as customers, suppliers, employees, and in processes, technology and innovation.

A key benefit of using the BSC framework is that it gives organisations a way to connect between the various components of strategic planning and management such that there will be a visible connection between the projects and programmes on which people are working, the measurements being used to track success, the strategic objectives the organisation is trying to accomplish and the mission, vision and strategy of the organisation.

Appendix 4: Enterprise Project Management Office (EPMO)

Functions of the EPMO are described in the next paragraphs.

Aligning the Portfolio to the Business Strategy

To ensure that all programmes and projects are aligned with the strategic direction of the company, after their selection, the Strategic PMO must vigilantly monitor and continually adjust the portfolio as risks escalate, opportunities arise and changes occur. Kathleen Hass, in her white paper, *From Strategy to Action: Enterprise Portfolio Management* (2005), pointedly states that "achieving organizational goals requires moving beyond strategic planning and conventional tactical approach to project management." PMI has found that 49% of organisations have an enterprise-wide PMO that is focused on improving the delivery of business strategy through portfolio management. Both PMI and PwC have found that organisations that align their overall strategies with their programme and project portfolios are more likely to have programmes and projects that meet schedule, scope, quality, budget and business benefits requirements.

Applications: It means that the PMO should ensure that the strategy developed for eliminating project failures and abandonment is rigorously aligned in the management of programmes and projects. Thus, the responses to risks and opportunities, check-and-balance systems, adaptive monitoring, etc., which are tactical in the implementation of the desired strategy should be consistently implemented in the management of the programmes and projects.

Customising Programme and Project Management Practices

The Strategic PMO can accomplish the first step of implementing OPM by taking into consideration the internal and external contexts of an organisation when defining a configuration of OPM that will deliver the most strategic value (Crawford & Cooke-Davies, 2012, p. 3). "Organizations adopting the surface appearances of implementation that worked for others, hoping that they will realize the same results, appear destined for disappointment" (Thomas & Mullaly, 2008, p. 360). Such organisations need to consider and address their internal strengths and weaknesses and their external commercial and political environments.

Application: In applying strategic solutions to solve our problems of project failures and abandonment, it is essential that companies should understand their internal strengths and weaknesses in order to adapt the proffered solutions to meet their needs. The applications should also be done with an eye on their impact on their environmental circumstances including political and economic. It is ill advised to make a blanket copy of what has worked for other companies without analysing how it will fit into your company.

Enhancing Governance and Accountability

The Strategic PMO is tasked with ensuring that all the programmes and projects are carried out in an effective and efficient manner. Confusion, caused by ambiguity, lack of accountability and poor coordination, is prevented when the Strategic PMO is accountable for the governance and leadership of the practices, roles and responsibilities, as well as driving integration of talent, processes and knowledge. Analysis of the PMI and PwC survey data reveals an undeniable positive correlation between having a Strategic PMO in place and better performance. The higher the alignment between the organisational strategy and business needs, the higher the overall project performance.

Optimising the Investment of Portfolio of Programmes and Projects

In order to optimise the efficiency and effectiveness of the portfolio of programmes and projects, the Strategic PMO must be involved in the following:

- Business decisions that result in new programmes and projects
- Strategic programme and project planning
- Setting of portfolio priorities
- Periodic programme and project reviews that result in decisions to discontinue programmes and projects (The PwC survey results highlight that programme and project selection was one of the most critical capabilities of the Strategic PMO.)

The Strategic PMO must also be committed to the continuous improvement in the practices of programme and project management, optimising the utilisation of resources and guaranteeing the delivery of the anticipated business results to maximise the organisation's investment in its portfolio of programmes and projects. With a PMO in place, PMI reported 4% fewer programmes and projects deemed failures, and 11% more programmes and projects met their business intent. In the same vein, PwC found that: "When an organization has a methodology in place to improve [programme and] project performance and management and focuses on continuous improvement, it will have a competitive advantage strategy in place to remain successful in the marketplace."

Managing Talent

Strategic PMOs recognise that engaging experienced key staff leads to programme and project success. After all, "Methodologies and processes don't deliver [programs and] projects; people do" (PwC). And "if an organization is to undertake all the [programs and] projects necessary to implement the chosen organizational strategy, there must be sufficient people with the right competences, skills, attitudes, and know-how to deliver the full portfolio" (Dinsmore & Cooke-Davies, 2006). This is why Strategic PMOs are investing in the development of their programme and project management competencies, providing access to training for their talent and identifying opportunities for career advancement within the organisation for those who want to grow.

Application: Training appropriate persons is essential, and retaining them in the organisation is equally important because this is one of the drawbacks many companies experience in Africa.

Ensuring Stakeholder Buy-In

The Strategic PMO is tasked with identifying and supporting stakeholders impacted by the programmes and projects in the portfolio to help them understand that the change is necessary and should contribute to the creation of sustained long-term value for the organisation. Evidence shows that the use of efficient and effective communication methodologies have a positive effect on the success of programmes and projects. It has been found that projects with efficient and effective communication methods were 17% more likely to finish within budget, according to PMI and PwC.

Driving Needed Change

The Strategic PMO engenders the driving and managing of organisational change through the portfolio of programmes and projects—ensuring that organisational change management becomes essential practice within OPM and helping organisations adapt to change, uncertainty and complexity. This ensures that the strategy is effectively implemented, and the expected benefits and changes are realised.

Proactively Navigating Risk

The Strategic PMO creates a culture of proactive risk management by the identification and navigation of threats as well as opportunities. "To achieve effective enterprise risk management, organizations must focus on being proactive, rather than merely reactive." The role of the Strategic PMO is to establish an integrated approach to risk management throughout the portfolio in order to support the organisation in delivering value and differentiation from competition.

OPM and the Strategic PMO are linked. OPM gives the organisation the capabilities to implement the delivery of its strategy, and a Strategic PMO moves beyond the traditional functions of a PMO with executive-level support to fit and implement OPM.

Appendix 5: Tips for PPM Success

- Robust and rigorous governance is critical to the success of an effective portfolio management organisation.
- It is critical to help enforce accountability, optimise cross-functional alignment and escalate issues to the appropriate decision makers.
- Strong governance can also help align communications, calendars and strategies across business units.
- It is essential to establish an unwavering financial discipline and regular reviews of portfolio performance throughout the entire process necessary to guide informed decisions.
- It is necessary to install standardised key performance indicators (KPIs) and powerful analytics to deliver objective insight for proactive decisions.
- Also essential is a benefits-realisation process that enables projects to yield the expected benefits and stop underperforming projects early.
- Inability to implement effective governance is a primary reason why companies fail to achieve best-in-class portfolio status, according to Aberdeen [1].

Some of the benefits of PPM Governance include the following:

- Proper governance will enable an EPMO to achieve better alignment with the business strategy and goals, along with an increased portfolio ROI and project success rate.
- It can help ensure the portfolio is managed optimally, from project selection to project closure.

- It will help manage the issue-escalation process. To escalate and resolve issues in a timely and efficient manner, portfolio leaders must develop an easy-to-follow issue-escalation process. They must also ensure that all stakeholders are aware of this process and agree to follow it. They must clearly identify stakeholders who have the responsibility for making decisions and define the escalation path for each issue. They should identify escalation dependencies such as tools, processes and people who must be involved. Predictability and repeatability should be incorporated into the process so that issues are resolved within a specific time frame with proper resolution communications.

- It will help install and maintain accountability. Project objectives should be aligned with the organisation's annual (and quarterly) performance goals, and portfolio success criteria are based on the business value. Accountability should empower the governance steering committee with the authority to make decisions and hold people answerable. People holding position-based roles and responsibilities should provide personal accountability. ROI and the percentage of projects on budget, for example, must be properly aligned with overall portfolio goals.

- It will facilitate communications. To enhance portfolio accountability, an enterprise-wide communications plan that promotes the performance and business value of portfolio management should be developed. Communication is critical because the scope of most portfolios could be distributed throughout the organisation and could be often global. An effective communications strategy must consistently articulate portfolio management goals, mission and vision. Communication plans should be centralised and customised for disparate stakeholder audiences and communicated via the appropriate channels.

- There should be centralised cross-functional coordination. The global nature of portfolios requires that EPMOs are fully aligned and coordinated across functions and divisions.

- There should be calendar alignment. Since portfolio projects are across multiple business units, it is necessary to align business unit calendars to ensure that the timings and movements are not delayed but synchronised.

- Effective PPM governance requires the automation of processes. To ensure prompt implementation, policies must be conveyed automatically through standard project management-automated communications tools. An example could be the use of existing workflow platforms such as Microsoft SharePoint where available.

■ There should be the use of KPIs. Leading EPMOs also tend to measure KPIs. They are used with performance management tools such as scorecards, dashboards and reports for reviewing a portfolio's relative health. The benefits of standardised KPIs include improved consistency across projects, better managed expectations and closer alignment of goals and accountabilities. Metrics can help ensure that appropriate levels of consistency and objectivity are applied when making decisions about an organisation's portfolio. Standardised, simplified KPIs also provide proactive insight into underperforming projects that enable management to take action during implementation. Because they are standardised, they can help PMO managers articulate to senior leadership the "big picture" rationale for portfolio decisions. Research demonstrates that investing adequate time upfront to standardise KPIs will bring substantial benefits later. For instance, Aberdeen has found that 67% of best-in-class companies use EPMOs standardised performance metrics to assess portfolio health and value, compared with an industry average of 39%.

■ PPM should invest in benefits-realisation metrics and manage them closely. Most companies use a rigorous process to review and accept projects based on financial benchmarks and business cases that promise enhanced productivity and cost savings. It is essential to assess and articulate the value and benefits that projects generate after implementation.

Benefits-realisation success metrics continuously track and manage the progress of benefits realisation and can easily identify poorly performing projects early on. And that makes it easier to manage risk and stop programmes and projects to avoid wasting additional resources. It is critical that the organisation implements a benefits-realisation process with regular reviews prior to the acceptance of a project. Thereafter, it is essential to maintain an unwavering focus on benefits realisation, whether the metrics are based on ROI, revenue generation, cost savings, quality, user adoption or some other value.

Reference

1. Aberdeen Group, "Project portfolio management: selecting the right projects for optimal investment opportunity." March 2011.

Appendix 6: Programme Benefits Management

The process includes the following processes:

- Process to clarify the programme's planned benefits and intended outcomes
- Processes to monitor the programme's ability to deliver the planned benefits and intended outcome

The purpose of Programme Benefits Management is to focus programme stakeholders on the outcomes and benefits of the various activities to be conducted during the programme's duration. Programme Benefits Management could consist of the following interactions:

- Benefits Identification
- Benefits Register
- Benefits Analysis and Planning
- Benefits Delivery
- Benefits Transition
- Benefits Sustainment

Benefits Identification

It is about identifying and qualifying the benefits that the programme intends or is expected to deliver. It is the starting point of the benefits management life cycle. It is all about identifying and qualifying the benefits that the program stakeholders are expecting the program to realise.

Its objective is to analyse all the available information about an organisation in order to identify and quantify the benefits that programme stakeholders expect to realise. During the organisational strategic planning, when the strategic objectives of an organisational initiative are identified, the benefits to be produced by the initiative in line with organisational corporate strategy are also identified by the programme governance unit which is the decision-making body. The body issues a programme mandate defining the initiative and the benefits. The important activities included in benefits identification are as follows:

Define high-level objectives: First, we need to define the high-level objectives and the Critical Success Factors (CSF) for the programme.

Identify business benefits: Identify specific business benefits and quantify them.

Delivery of objectives: How the objectives translate into benefits and in what quantities.

Develop KPI's: Developing metrics and KPIs to measure actual delivery of benefits and planned benefits.

These are necessary to baseline the expectations of benefits realisation.

Establish specific processes: Specific processes are to be established for each of the identified benefits at an early stage and for monitoring, tracking and communicating the planned and realised benefits.

As the benefits are identified, they must be captured in the benefits register.

Benefits Register

It is created during the benefits identification stage and updated and refined and is based on the programme strategic objectives and the business case. Its benefits include the following:

- It collects and lists the planned benefits from a programme. The more comprehensive the list, the more complete will be the overall benefits management activity within the programme.
- It is used to monitor, measure and communicate the delivery of benefits throughout the duration.
- It contains the key performance indicators (KPIs) that measure the benefits.
- It contains the thresholds for the benefits. By setting the thresholds, we can monitor the minimum expectations to each benefit

- It specifies how a benefit may be measured.
- It maps the planned benefits to programme components such that it is able to trace which components, and which specific activities within the components of a programme are responsible for realising a benefit.
- It shows the ownership of each benefit.
- It contains status indicator which displays performance of the various components.
- It contains significant milestones for the achievement of the benefits showing when a benefit will start, when it is delivered, etc.
- It identifies stakeholders responsible for delivering the benefits.
- It is normally reviewed with key stakeholders to develop appropriate performance for each of the benefits.

Composition of the benefit register: It comprises the following:

- A list of planned benefits
- Linking the planned benefits with the programme components as indicated in the programme roadmap
- A description of how each of the benefits will be measured
- The derived KPIs and their respective thresholds for measuring their achievements
- Status or progress indicator for each benefit
- Target dates and milestones for benefits achievement
- Responsible person or team for delivering each benefit

Benefits Analysis and Planning

With benefits defined, we need to establish how they will be achieved. The programme manager has to define and prioritise the components according to their contributions to the planned benefits. Appropriate metrics that will help derive the benefits are defined. In effect, this is where the benefits realisation plan is established, and the metrics and measurement framework for tracking the benefits are created. Its activities include the following:

- It identifies programme components
- It establishes the plan to realise the benefits by identifying the programme components that produce the benefits.
- It defines priorities in line with the expectations and timelines for benefits delivery.

- It defines the KPIs and establishes the process for measurement of the benefits.
- It examines the feasibility of realising the expected benefits and establishes a performance baseline with regard to the benefits.
- It establishes a connection between the benefits realisation plan and the roadmap of the programme, i.e., at what point in the roadmap the benefits will be realised. It also needs to establish a link between the benefits and the plans of the various components.
- It ensures that as the tasks of the components are completed, they should contribute to the realisation of the benefits.
- It creates a plan for transition and sustainment of benefits over a long term.

Benefits Realisation Plan

A benefits realisation plan is established showing how, when and in what quantities the benefits will be delivered and monitored.

The benefits will be mapped to the overall programme management plan. Delivery and planning activities are cyclical.

The benefits realisation plan formally documents the activities necessary to achieve the planned benefits from the programme. It should achieve the following purposes:

- It defines the benefits and how they will be achieved.
- It should link the outputs of specific components clearly to the programme outcomes.
- It should define the metrics for measurement of the benefits.
- It should define the roles and responsibilities of the overall benefits management process.
- It should define how the benefits will be transitioned and sustained such as who will receive them and how they will be sustained.
- It should establish a process to monitor the extent to which a programme is able to meet the desired benefits.

Benefits Delivery

The programme manager monitors the components, to ensure that they are contributing to the benefits. A benefits register will be maintained and there will be report on the benefits being delivered.

Activities during the benefits delivery stage are as follows:

- The programme monitors the external and internal environment of an organisation and maps it to the programme's objectives and benefits.
- It initiates, performs, transitions and closes the components in line with the programme management plan and manages the interdependencies between the components.
- It ensures that the timetable for initiating, performing, transitioning and closing has to be mapped to the benefits timetable.
- It evaluates the risks to the realisation of the benefits and their key performance indicators.
- It records the progress of the benefits realised in the benefits register and reports to the stakeholders in line with the communication plan.
- It initiates components and integrates the output of the components to realise the benefits as planned.
- It monitors and ensures that the accumulated and attainable benefits are in line with the expectations and the overall strategy of the organisation.

From benefits delivered to benefits transition.

Benefits Transition

Benefits transition consolidates the coordinated benefits and transfers the ongoing responsibility of the benefits to a receiving organisation.

In benefits transition, the programme needs to ensure that the benefits produced in the programme are transitioned smoothly. The recipient of the benefits from the programme is typically an operational unit (such as sales or service). The key consideration in transitioning is to ensure that the benefits realisation will be sustained. The process of transition should start before the programme closes and continues even after the programme closes.

During the transition, the programme should evaluate the actual vs. planned benefits to see how successful the programme has been in benefits realisation. If the realisation and transition of benefits require integration of the output of various components, then the work must be completed successfully before the transition.

The programme should make sure that if the transition requires changes to be made in the operational unit, there is enthusiasm and willingness to make those changes.

The programme should assess the readiness and approval of the receiving person or organisation (in terms of availability of resources, capabilities and infrastructure), to take over the benefits sustainment responsibility. During the transition, the programme will gradually release the resources. It is possible that some of these resources will also be transferred to the receiving organisation during the transition.

In the next section of the programme benefits management tutorial, we will look into benefits sustainment.

Benefits Sustainment

During and after the transition, there should be arrangements for continued benefits sustainment. These will include the following:

- Arrangements for active monitoring and measurement of the performance of benefits on a long-term basis.
- Establishment of the infrastructure for continuous realisation of the programme benefits over a long term.

Moving beyond transition, the benefits sustainment step refers to ensuring the sustenance of benefits long after the programme is closed.

It is important to understand that it is the responsibility of the programme to ensure that provisions for long-term sustenance are made. The responsibility for monitoring the ongoing benefits sustenance then transfers over to the receiving organisation.

This provision includes a plan for the changes necessary to the operations; any financing and behavioural changes necessary to continue performance monitoring (including training and enablement) are made.

The programme should provide the resources (for example, people, a supply of spares, etc.) and budget necessary for sustaining the benefits. The programme should provide the framework to monitor the performance of the outcome of the plan.

It should also monitor the continued suitability of the product or service, as the business environment changes.

Summary of Benefits Realisation Management (BRM)

Benefits realisation management incorporates the activities of managing benefits throughout the life of the project and consists of Identify, Execute and Sustain.

- **Identify benefits:** to determine whether projects, programmes and portfolios can produce the intended business results.
- **Execute benefits management:** to minimise risks to future benefits and maximise the opportunity to gain additional benefits.
- **Sustain benefits realisation:** to ensure that whatever the project or programme produces continues to create value (post-implementation).

It is helpful to explore the activities in each of these areas.

Identify Benefits

- Before the start of the project, identify benefits in the business case development.
  - Define key performance indicators and quantitative measures to track benefits.
  - Establish processes for measuring progress against benefits realisation plan.
  - Create a communications plan necessary to record progress and report to stakeholders.

Execute Benefits Management

- Establish a benefits realisation plan. A benefits realisation plan outlines the activities necessary for achieving the planned benefits. It identifies a timeline and the tools and resources necessary to ensure the benefits are fully realised over time.
  - Define key performance indicators and quantitative measures to track benefits. Measuring the progress of benefits throughout the project life cycle can also guard against scope creep.
  - Monitor and control the project to ensure that it remains aligned with the organisation's strategic objectives.
  - Track and report project progress to key stakeholders as per the communications management plan.

Sustain Benefits Realisation

- Transition the project deliverables to the business.
  - Maintain strong cross-functional communications, engagement and sharing of lessons learned.

- Monitor and measure benefits performance and reporting results to key stakeholders.
- Support users and develop business cases for future initiatives to address operational needs.

Responsibility for BRM

Even though benefits are realised on the business/operations side of the organisation, benefits realisation management is a shared responsibility between project managers, business owners, executive sponsors and senior leaders, even when a dedicated *benefits owner* is appointed for the project.

The continuity from project to operations can be achieved by embedding someone from the operations or strategy development team into the project team or transitioning some project team members into operational roles.

Role of Project Manager in BRM

Benefits realisation is a central component of project and programme management. Project managers are in a unique position to help their customers gain the benefits detailed in the business case. Emphasis should be put on engaging project managers early in the discussions around benefits analysis, alignment of projects with business strategy. The idea is that when project managers participate in such discussions, they are more likely to focus on creation of business value rather than keeping a narrow focus on project deliverables and traditional measures of success (such as on time and on budget).

Before Project Initiation

■ Collaborate with executive leaders and business owners in the identification of benefits as part of the business case development.

During Project Initiation

■ Validate benefits and their alignment to organisational strategy.

During Project Planning

■ Create a benefits realisation plan.
 – Define key performance indicators and quantitative measures to track benefits.
 – Establish processes for measuring progress against benefits realisation plan.
 – Create a communications plan necessary to record progress and report to stakeholders.

During Project Execution, Monitoring and Controlling

■ Monitor whether the project is on course to deliver the expected benefits.
 – Track metrics, flag and manage emerging risks and communicate the information that executive leaders need in order to decide the future of a project if targeted benefits are in jeopardy or no longer relevant.
 – Fully understand the operational realities (such as operability, maintainability, total cost of ownership, etc.)

During Closure

■ Transition the project deliverables to business/operations. This includes knowledge transfer to business to help them derive maximum benefits from the deliverables and avoid potential issues.
 – Share lessons learned that could impact future deliverables.
 – Update the benefits realisation plan. Note that benefits realisation plan may continue to be updated during the sustainment phase.

Role of Leadership in BRM

Executive leaders play a critical role in creating a successful benefits management culture. They set the tone at the top by emphasising the value of BRM. They embed that value into the organisation's culture and assign responsibility for benefits management to leaders and their teams—on both the project and operations sides of their businesses.

Conclusion

Benefits realisation is a key to achieving organisation's strategic business goals or objectives. Projects and programmes are primary vehicles to deliver the benefits to help meet those strategic goals. Organisations that use formal project management for benefits realisation management tend to be more successful in delivering value. Benefits realisation is a shared responsibility between project managers, business owners, executive sponsors and senior leaders [1].

Discussion on Benefit Realisation Management

During the Oracle Engineering and Construction Conference, 10 to 11 October 2017, in London, we looked at the cost of operation and maintenance of the deliverable after it has been handed over. It has been suggested that the cost of the operation might be as much as 20 times the cost of the project which covers the cost of initiation, planning, execution and handover. There was an opportunity to discuss with a project manager (name withheld) of the Cement Division of FLSmidth A/S. FLSmidth & Co. is a global engineering company based in Copenhagen, Denmark. With almost 13,000 employees worldwide, it provides global cement and mineral industries with factories, machinery, services and know-how. The company designs, manufactures and supplies production plants, equipment, single machinery and spare parts primarily to the cement and minerals industries.

In our conversation, he explained that the cement factories they build for customers could have a lifetime of operations of 20 to 30 or more years. He also confirmed that one of the factories they built in Angola failed just after five years because of poor maintenance.

It is certainly a large fund required to plan to maintain and operate such a plant for 20 to 30 years. This suggests that the cost of lifecycle design, implementation, operation and maintenance should be huge [2].

However, if it is planned that the project deliverable starts generating income when it is commissioned, then it may be feasible to factor such incomes into the cost of maintenance of the taken-over deliverable.

References

1. Nick Castlelinna, "Research director, business planning and execution." Aberdeen Group.
2. Harwinder Singh, "What is benefits realization management (BRM)?" Project Management Examination Preparation App, BrainBok Company, 6 November 2016.

Appendix 7: Key Performance Index (KPI)

How to Write and Develop KPIs

When writing or developing a KPI, you need to consider how that KPI relates to a specific business outcome or objective. KPIs need to be customised to your business situation and should be developed to help you achieve your goals. Follow these steps when writing a KPI:

- Write a clear objective for your KPI
- Share your KPI with stakeholders
- Review the KPI on a weekly or monthly basis
- Make sure the KPI is actionable
- Evolve your KPI to fit the changing needs of the business
- Check to see that the KPI is attainable
- Update your KPI objectives as needed

Features of good KPIs:

- Provide an objective way to see if our strategy is working
- Offer a comparison that gauges the degree of performance change over time
- Focus employees' attention on what matters most to success
- Allow measurement of accomplishments, not just of the work that is performed
- Provide a common language for communication
- Help reduce intangible uncertainty
- Are valid, to ensure measurement of the right things
- Are verifiable, to ensure data collection accuracy

Appendix 8: Balanced Scorecard (BSC)

In organisational strategy management, a system could be chosen that gives a linkage between the balanced scorecard (BSC) and KPI. Before discussing this linkage, it is relevant to touch a bit on the balanced scorecard.

The balanced scorecard is a strategic planning and management system used in global businesses, industries, government and non-profit organisations to align business activities to their visions and strategies. It is used to improve internal and external communications and monitor organisational performance against strategic goals. It helps organisations to establish how operational activities link to the strategy and provide measurable impact [1].

It is a management system (not only a measurement system) that enables organisations to clarify their vision and strategy and translate them into action. It provides feedback around both the internal business processes and the external outcomes in order to improve strategic performance and results continuously. When fully deployed, the balanced scorecard transforms strategic planning from an academic exercise into the nerve centre of an enterprise. It constitutes a framework that not only provides performance measurements but helps planners identify what should be done and measured. It enables executives to truly execute their strategies.

Cascading the BSC

Cascading a balanced scorecard means to translate the corporate-wide scorecard (referred to as **Tier 1**) down to first business units, support units or departments (**Tier 2**) and then teams or individuals (**Tier 3**). The end result should be focused across all levels of the organisation that is

235

consistent. The organisation alignment should be clearly visible through strategy, using the strategy map, performance measures and targets and initiatives. Scorecards should be used to improve accountability through objective and performance measure ownership, and desired employee behaviours should be incentivised with recognition and rewards.

Cascading strategy focuses the entire organisation on strategy and creating line-of-sight between the work people do and high-level desired results. As the management system is cascaded down through the organisation, objectives become more operational and tactical, as do the performance measures. Accountability follows the objectives and measures, as ownership is defined at each level. An emphasis on results and the strategies needed to produce results is communicated throughout the organisation. This alignment step is critical to becoming a strategy-focused organisation.

Operations of the BSC

While traditionally companies used only short-term financial performance as measure of success, the "balanced scorecard" added additional non-financial strategic measures to the system in order to better focus on long-term success. The system has evolved over the years into a fully integrated strategic management system.

Recognising some of the weaknesses and vagueness of previous management approaches, the balanced scorecard approach provides a clear prescription as to what companies should measure in order to "balance" the financial perspective.

A key benefit of using the BSC framework is that it gives organisations a way to connect between the various components of strategic planning and management such that there will be a visible connection between the projects and programmes that people are working on, the measurements being used to track success, the strategic objectives the organisation is trying to accomplish and the mission, vision and strategy of the organisation.

Reference

1. "The institute way: simplify strategic planning & management with the balanced scorecard," 2016.

Appendix 9: Enterprise Risk Management

Definition

Enterprise Risk Management (ERM) could be defined as the process of planning, organising, leading and controlling the activities of an organisation in order to minimise the effects of risk on its operations, capital and earnings.

It enables the systematic identification, balancing and controlling of portfolio of business risks and the alignment of an organisation's risk profile with its risk appetite.

An effective Enterprise Risk Management programme engenders informed decision-making, which leads to success in the form of better performance and greater rewards.

It transforms the organisation and enables the addressing of the organisation's risks potential. Thus, it is feasible to identify, understand and manage risks to achieve sustainable and long-term growth.

An effective Enterprise Risk Management programme will help achieve the following in an organisation:

- Establish the foundation for the collation of all risk data
- Expose and facilitate the visibility for all risk data
- Enhance risk accountability and control
- Ensure compliance with existing and new regulations and frameworks

Effective Risk Management helps the creation of a competitive advantage that facilitates growth. It is stated by The Swiss ReGroup: "In 2011, total economic losses due to disasters reached a record $350 billion (USD) with only $108 billion (USD) covered by insurance exposing those affected to almost 70% of all losses – directly impacting their bottom line" [1].

An Enterprise Risk Management should cover all enterprise risks which include Operational Risk, Project Risk Management, Governance and Compliance Risk and Opportunity Risk as listed below.

Operational Risk Management includes the following:

- Strategic Risk Management
- Supply Chain Risk
- Incident Management
- Health and Safety
- Business Development
- Business Continuity, etc.

Project Risk Management

- Project and Program Risk Management
- Portfolio Management
- Schedule Risk Management
- Change Management
- Progress Management, etc.

Governance and Compliance Risk

- Business Ethics
- Internal Risk Audit
- IT Security
- Corporate Governance
- Compliance Management, etc.

Opportunity Management

- Innovation
- New Markets
- New Product Development
- Business Process Improvement
- Cost Savings
- Margin Improvement, etc.

Anti-bribery and anti-corruption (ABAC) risk assessment process should be carried out within the ERM framework. The framework provides a framework to understand and respond to business uncertainties and opportunities with relevant risk insight delivered through common, integrated risk identification, analysis and management disciplines.

Design and Implementation of an ERM Framework

For an organisation to identify and list its risk appetite, it should first determine its goals and objectives and its business strategy. It should define what it wants to achieve in terms of markets, geographies, segments, products, earnings and so on. With this done, it can assess the risks implied in that strategy and determine the level of risk it is willing to assume in executing that strategy.

ERM helps an organisation evolve from a siloed risk approach to a broader view of understanding and practice of risk management including its rewards and trade-offs.

An Enterprise Risk Management strategy should include identifying sources of risks, categorising and analysing the risks, evaluating the risks and installing the framework which should be an effective ongoing procedure for managing and controlling the risks.

There is no one-size-fits-all approach to ERM; the design of an ERM programme and its implementation strategy should complement the organisation's culture and support its ERM goals. Project teams should develop tailored ERM strategies in their applications. An ERM framework should leverage existing organisational structures and processes and incorporate external best practices.

The recommended approach should be to understand the specific issues impacting the organisation and then to design bespoke solutions to address the hierarchy of risks.

The ERM concept is that risks that affect and could affect an organisation are of different nature and their sum does not give the total risk. Several correlations should be considered when different risks are aggregated.

ERM is a rigorous approach to assessing and addressing the risks from all sources that threaten the achievement of an organisation's strategic objectives.

The first step in implementing ERM is to identify the risks the organisation is exposed to. A common approach is to identify the types of risks that will be measured. There could be a phased and structured approach to implementing ERM so that organisations can develop baseline frameworks that could be expanded and enhanced over time.

Steps for Implementing ERM

It is suggested that ERM could be implemented step by step by using the blocks in the framework as follows (Figure A.1):

1. Identify: Identify and list the risks to which the organisation is exposed. Also, list the business needs that could be met through a structured ERM approach.
2. Analyse: It is necessary to do a root-cause analysis of risks.
3. Control:
   - Define the Steps.
   - Try to unite and work together with anyone who has the responsibility for risk mitigation in any discipline in the company. Executive sponsors should be helpful. Knowledgeable and influential people who have access to the board should be helpful in the team.
   - The scope of an enterprise-wide risk management assignment may appear daunting, but it is wise and pragmatic to break the assignment into achievable objectives.

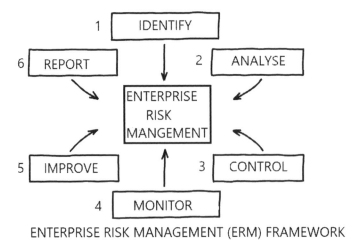

ENTERPRISE RISK MANAGEMENT (ERM) FRAMEWORK

Figure A.1   Enterprise Risk Management Framework.

- Assign the task in each area to a specific person. Parameters should be set for success, and the time limits should be set for the implementation of the achievable objective in each area.
- It is not realistic and possible to attend to every risk immediately. Start with those that matter most for the success of the organisation's strategic objectives. This means that the risks should be prioritised in line with company's objectives. This underscores the importance of an executive sponsor who could help to advise on the organisation's priorities.
- Name an owner for each risk. The person should be responsible for managing and monitoring the risk to ensure that it is being mitigated. The risk owner could be someone working in the function or task which could be at risk.

4. Monitor:
   - Manage accountability
   - The risk owners should include in their normal business reports updates on key issues as the risk targets and monitored reading of the risk status and specific activities that have taken place since the last report.
   - Challenges in executing the risk plan and a trend assessment in the risk profile against the targeted outcome.

5. Improve:
   - Streamline and enhance the process.
   - Ensure performance and visibility.

6. Report on progress: Periodic reports to senior management on the progress of ERM programme should include progress related to milestones for specific ERM objectives.

Acknowledgement

Some information in this appendix has been adapted from the Active Risk Group and modified for this publication [2].

References

1. The Swiss ReGroup, "Natural and man-made catastrophes in 2011 report."
2. "Embrace risk," a publication of the Active Risk Group.

Index